SHAKESPEAREAN WIG STYLING
A Practical Guide to Wig Making
for the 1500s–1600s

SHAKESPEAREAN WIG STYLING
A Practical Guide to Wig Making
for the 1500s–1600s

Brenda Leedham and Lizzee Leedham

THE CROWOOD PRESS

First published in 2021 by
The Crowood Press Ltd
Ramsbury, Marlborough
Wiltshire SN8 2HR

enquiries@crowood.com

www.crowood.com

British Library Cataloguing-in-Publication Data
A catalogue record for this book is available from the
British Library.

ISBN 978 1 78500 882 5

Front cover design by Maggie Mellett
Photography by Lizzee Leedham
Illustrations by Will Peart and Sophie Wright
Frontispiece: Photo manipulation by Rachel Bywater

Typeset by Sharon Dainton Design
Printed and bound in India by Parksons Graphics Pvt Ltd.

'And this our life, exempt from public
haunt, finds tongues in trees, books in
the running brooks, sermons in stones,
and good in everything. I would not
change it.'

William Shakespeare, *As You Like It*

Contents

Acknowledgements

We would first like to thank The Crowood Press for giving us the opportunity to write this book.

Thanks to The Royal Shakespeare Company, whose productions have inspired us and without which we would not have joined the worldwide family of Wiggies.

The Shakespeare Birthplace Trust has been hugely supportive, encouraging us to give talks and demonstrations about Shakespearean wigs in theatre to groups from all over the world. The archives at the Shakespeare Birthplace Trust hold many historical items and manuscripts, paintings and photographs, their own records and those of the Royal Shakespeare Theatre.

Personal thanks from Brenda go to Felicite Gillham who welcomed her to her first wig room and Kenneth Lintott, the creative presiding genius, for the opportunities and the patient, thorough training they gave.

From Lizzee: Thanks go to my mother for her unflinching love and support, her dedication to the theatre, which has sustained our family, and far-reaching wisdom, which still astonishes me daily. Thanks to the RSC Wig Department for the memories, training, opportunities and love.

Thanks to my best friend, Bethany Jane Davies, vintage hair extraordinaire and Fatale Cosmetics CEO, for everything.

Thanks also to Will Peart for the brilliant illustrations and sense of humour. I wish we could have had far more of your illustrations.

Thanks to Scott Hazell, AKA Casta Hex, for their makeup, modelling and photography skills.

Thanks also to Dawn, Jonathan and Zoe, dear family friends and gracious models for the hair prep, wig cap and shell sections.

Thank you to the entertainers and writers who inspire us all, celebrating life and fantasy in all their wonder and diversity.

Thanks also go to you, the reader. You are continuing a craft almost as old as humanity itself. Your knowledge and experience will be added to ours as you read and create so please make use of the margins for your notes and ideas. Thank you for climbing the ever-higher Wiggy pyramid of knowledge, topping it with the flourish that only you can provide. You will be part of something greater than yourself which brings joy, education and entertainment to all; shares a sense of time and culture; and can shield us, if temporarily, from the world's slings and arrows.

The Royal Shakespeare Theatre, 2011, attributed to David Dixon.

Preface

ABOUT THE AUTHORS

Brenda Leedham was head of the wigs and make-up department at the Royal Shakespeare Theatre from 1974 to 2007. Since 'retiring' she has continued to educate in demonstrations and is happily working with Leedham Wigs, now owned by her daughter, Lizzee Leedham.

As a freelance wig maker, she has worked for TV, opera and ballet companies, on musicals and films, made wigs for the National Trust, private individuals, dolls, ventriloquist dummies, costumed museum mannequins and dead heads (fake, of course).

Lizzee Leedham is co-author, co-editor and photographer for this book. Her earliest memories are of the wig room at the RSC and touring the country listening to the theatrical wigs and make-up talks given by Brenda. She was trained in each skill as soon as physically able, although she resisted the lure of the theatre. Instead, she completed her MA and taught GCSE and A level English for twelve years, becoming a teacher training specialist and creating teaching resources for a wide range of texts. After years of part-time wig making and taking on the role of model and co-presenter of our demonstrations, Lizzee took over Leedham Wigs full time in 2019, expanding the business online and into selling, not only renting out, our custom creations.

PERSONAL PROFILES

Brenda Leedham

After studying Theatre Craft and Design, I spent a year at Goldsmiths College, starting a degree in Speech and Drama in Education. I worked every weekend at the Royal Shakespeare Theatre in Stratford-upon-Avon and hoped that this was my future, not teaching and putting on the school play. The moment full-time work was offered, I left London for Stratford-upon-Avon. At Stratford-upon-Avon I assisted in the wig room, where staff worked as a team, sharing their skills in hairdressing, wig making, prosthetics and make-up, maintaining the current shows and preparing the new ones. It smelled of hairspray and Brilliantine.

Although I had visited the make-up room of a TV company in Birmingham and helped with costume and props backstage in several theatres, I had only noticed the costumes and scenery, I had no idea so many wigs, hairpieces, prosthetics and facial hair were in use. That, of course, is the idea.

Luckily, at that time, enthusiasm and availability were the only qualifications necessary for a general assistant, but a long and thorough training in all aspects of the work followed.

I was taught, coached and mentored by experts Kenneth Lintott, Felicite Gillham and Cathy Buchwald, and was able to put into practice the skills as I acquired them, building my confidence. I used my holidays and any spare time to make wigs. Ken gave me work making postiche and prosthetics for films and TV, Gillie and Cathy took me to theatres all over the country working on wigs, hair and make-up.

Brenda Leedham and Lizzee Leedham, backstage at The Talisman Theatre, Kenilworth, 2019.

As I gained the confidence of designers, they commissioned work directly and I made prosthetics and postiche for Scottish Opera, Payne's Plough, ENO, the Northern College of Music and so many more organizations than there is room to list here.

I toured as wig mistress to Paris during the riots of 1968 and across Europe, even to Japan.

When I became wig mistress, I accepted visits to the department from schools, taught in colleges and promoted the opportunities for our work in TV and newspaper interviews.

I am still demonstrating and talking about wigs and make-up in theatre with my daughter at Shakespeare's Birthplace and the RSC, long after my promised retirement. Why stop doing what you love?

Lizzee Leedham

Imposter Syndrome is a well-documented issue in creative industries. My mother and I both have it. No doubt, unless you are very confident, you will feel some sense of trepidation when meeting new clients and trying new projects, no matter what your prior experience; after all, the tools, techniques and people change and you will always be learning and pushing yourself – but that is in itself one of the great joys of this industry. You may love working with actors in person or work more remotely. You may find yourself in a bustling backstage theatre environment, a humid film trailer, a wet Welsh field and an extravagant wedding all in the same week.

Having grown up backstage at the Royal Shakespeare Theatre and taken on as many work experience opportunities there as possible, I knew the gruelling schedule came with, for me, anxiety-induced night-terrors even on low-risk productions. There are a whole host of far more personal and holistic duties which theatre Wiggies must be ready to perform. Due to the pressures of live performances, many theatre actors are simmering with adrenaline, making them a little unpredictable (and sweaty).

After qualifying as an English teacher, I still returned home to work with Mum on productions during holidays, completing piece work remotely. My almost-sister, Bethany Jane Davies, came to speak at a student careers event. She explained how her hairdressing qualifications had led her to specialize in vintage hair and make-up. Her brand, *The Vintage Beauty Parlour*, had successfully opened a bricks and mortar premises on her doorstep, she had written a book (also published by Crowood – *Vintage Hairstyles of the 1940s*) and had an online following of thousands from around the world. She talked about the importance of finding a

Lizzee Leedham and Bethany Jane Davies. Hair by Bethany Jane Davies.

job for your lifestyle and your passions. She is now CEO of Fatale Cosmetics and continues to inspire. It occurred to me only at this point that the skills I already had could provide me with an income on a self-employed basis. How appealing that idea became over the years!

Mum had started up a wig rental business, providing wigs to local theatres after leaving the RSC and was doing well, but that meant she needed an extra pair of hands.

As a now ex-teacher, I had an empathetic soul and plentiful time in which to knot and watch my favourite

shows with a wiser eye. For example, I had been watching *RuPaul's Drag Race* for several years and just had to experiment with synthetic hair and frames. This appealed partly because it was a new set of techniques to learn and tools to work with and partly because I could see the empowering personal and political potential of the art burgeoning. Once I realized there was a gap in the market providing facial hair for kings, I took the helm, diversifying our clients and broadening our reach online. Leedham Wigs is now supporting a blossoming drag royalty scene as well as the private individuals alongside the production companies we supported before.

As with many careers now, we must be ready and willing to be flexible and adapt. Indeed, between the first and final drafts of this book, Covid-19 has forced massive changes including a period of lockdown. At the first draft, the theatres, tourist attractions, film and television production companies and even schools cancelled their rented wig bookings and our talks and demonstrations. The pubs and bars that showcased performers also closed, forcing independent entertainers online. Yet, with lockdown, came an increase in demand for these live performances and wider audiences necessitated a wider range of looks for performers. A growing drag scene with new performers needed somewhere to style, repair and customize the now cheap and readily available lace-front synthetic wigs available to buy online, so we were able to increase this side of the business.

National and international theatres are, at the time of writing, showing productions live outdoors to combat the risk of infection (much of this, as Shakespeare fans, feels very authentic) or showing the productions online either live or pre-recorded. Individual performers have slayed audiences from their windows in the streets, socially distanced in car parks and invited us into their homes as once entertainers would have arrived in market squares, village greens and the yards of public houses.

The more things change, the more they will seem the same. Unpredictability is a part of life. Whichever way your wig-making career takes you, I hope you will never tire of seeing your creations make a character, creature, or person come to life.

Feel free to take our advice along with that of others, disregard what doesn't work for you, and enjoy the moment.

Introduction

This book aims to provide a stepping-stone as you emerge from training into professional work in the industry. An extra source of information as you set up your wig-making enterprise. We are here to refresh, in detail, the wig-making and wig-styling skills you have learned but are perhaps not yet confident enough to advertise.

As a jumping-off point, we shall look at some of Shakespeare's plays and characters in the context of the history of the sixteenth and seventeenth centuries, specifically at several styles in each century for men and women, and follow the construction of each one through from design to finished look.

With each wig there will be details of the circumstances of performance given in NOTES.

Obstacles to overcome and challenges for the wig maker to solve include the costume's interference, time limitations, changes and so on, followed by a choice of materials and techniques to tackle these. These challenges are the sort that will transfer to all your work in media.

Chapters 4, 5, 7 and 8 will guide you through a range of construction and styling techniques which, while they may not cover every character explicitly, cover a range of archetypal characters with similar needs to many others. Wigs can last seasons or become working parts, being adapted and transformed into many wigs over many decades.

TRAINING

Today, there are excellent courses in media skills all over the country.

A series of practical skills in hairdressing, wig-making and make-up are required by the industry, so the length of a course is often a good way to assess its value. The longer degree courses generally offer more opportunity to become adept and to produce a good portfolio of examples to show employers. Shorter courses transmit the knowledge, but do not allow the time for those skills to be practised and developed.

The larger colleges provide realistic experience alongside other trainee theatre and media students. Most will produce shows, displays and short films to showcase their students' work. Some colleges offer contacts for professional work experience, but in all of them you are getting to know your fellow future media workers. This network may help you find work later.

The greatest advantage is that they will guide you through obtaining industry-recognized qualifications such as City and Guilds of London Institute, advanced wig making and hairdressing. The greatest difficulty is often financial, not just finding the course fees in advance, but during the course, buying wig-making tools, wig lace, hair, prosthetic materials, make-up supplies, and reference books.

Some choose to follow a series of short, intensive courses as the money becomes available and practise at home between courses. These short courses are designed and run by industry professionals. They can give the most up-to-date information on products and techniques. Smaller groups mean you will have more opportunity to impress these useful contacts with your skills, enthusiasm and diligence.

A newly qualified wig maker may have to find other types of work and part-time opportunities before beginning full-time work in their chosen career. However, nothing is wasted. Maturity and the experience of working professionally in almost any field will be an asset.

LEFT: Casta Hex as Elizabeth I in a sixteenth-century wig. Make up, model, photography by Scott Hazell (2020).

The Work of the Wig Maker

This chapter covers advertising your skills, developing your skills, the work of a wig maker in a wig-making business or in a theatre and a timeline to ensure you meet your many and varied deadlines.

ONGOING WORK

1. Advertise Your Skills and Contact Details

You are now a brand and must have a professional front to put on. Wig Maker, or Hair and Make-Up Artist, followed by name and contact details should be seen loud and clear. Your work portfolio should be easy for clients to find online. Keep your digital platform landing page brief. Make your contact details obvious, and accurate. A missing digit from your mobile number or a change of email address will lose you an offer.

The same applies to your CV, preferably just one page, kept concise and accurate. You will be one of many applicants for any position, so begin with your most relevant experience and qualifications. Then double-check for grammar, spelling and accuracy.

2. Update Your Online Sites and CV Regularly

Web pages and cards must be updated as you gain enough professional experience to call yourself Wig Designer or apply for work as Wig Supervisor. You will find daily social media presence will help too.

3. Practice

Set up a workspace and collect enough 'tools of the trade' to work with at home. There is much more detail on this in Chapter 3. Hone those skills in any way you can afford. For practical skills, you need to develop muscle memory and must begin to pick up speed if you hope to work commercially. Rather than full-size wigs, make smaller items, partly to save money on materials, but also in order that each working step becomes clearly understood and automatic. There are lots of techniques mentioned in this book such as taking a shell, wrapping hair and gripping wig caps which can be practised easily at home on a wig and block or on volunteers.

4. Develop Extra Skills

Practise whatever skill is affordable and enjoyable in your spare time. Consider some of the following:

- Punching a bald cap or prosthetic ears, or implanting hair in wax.
- Buying cheaper fibre party wigs and adding lace fronts to them.
- Designing and making frames to style eye-catching fantasy wigs.
- Knot toupees and toppers.

Put only the best pictures and film of your work on social media. Take your samples to industry fairs, contact drama groups and networking websites, sell at cosplay and re-enactors fairs. If you find a good niche, you may have found a new income stream!

5. Make Over Your Friends

Doing the work on yourself is not the same as working on other people or enough to develop your skills. Knotting ability does not make you a wig maker; the wig is not complete until styled and ready to use. Practise your hairdressing on friends, family, the delivery person, as well as on wigs. Treat it as an opportunity to develop people skills and to learn to work quickly while chatting casually.

WIG-MAKING EMPLOYMENT ROLES

To begin, alongside starting your own business, apply for every vacancy in wig-related work. They are rare. Short-term, part-time vacancies are less likely to attract experienced professionals, so your competition will be newcomers like yourself.

1. In a Wig-Making Business

If you are accepted as a trainee or part-time assistant in an established wig-making business, you will primarily be

LEFT: Knotting at a workstation in the corner of a wig room.

knotting backs of wigs, freeing up the more experienced makers to do foundations, fronts and partings. You may also be blocking up, cleaning and combing out wigs.

This work will be on the stock wigs so your starting skill level can be assessed. You may be required to sign a form that you will not use the training they give you to work for a rival company or indeed yourself.

If all goes well, expect to be given more responsibility when they have busy periods and be first in line for full-time work when the opportunity presents itself.

You will work in-house so that your work can be supervised, and training given. If they are impressed with your work, and if there is a vacancy, you may become one of their senior wig makers, knotting the more delicate laces and making foundations. At this point, you may be able to choose to work from home, collecting and delivering work from their premises.

Finally, a position with responsibility for fitting and supervising the making and finishing of complete wigs for their clients may become available. Some wig-making businesses offer internships. Search them out! These are rare opportunities to work with your fellow professionals and although you may not be paid much, you will be building your skills and portfolio.

2. Out Knotter

Some organizations will take on out knotters. This work is usually short-term and offered first to people whose standard of work they are familiar with, such as an ex-member of the department or someone who has been recommended to them.

You will be given a foundation, already made and fitted. The hair is supplied with a design and detailed instructions and delivery date. You will be trusted to work at home, alone, to a professional standard and deliver the item on time. It should go without saying that you should not eat, drink or smoke near the workroom for fear of the hair being contaminated. You will not be expected to cut or style the wig.

The fee will vary with the work and as there is competition for this type of work, it is often not negotiable. However, for knotting a complete lace-fronted wig, expect to receive the equivalent of a week's pay for an assistant wig and make-up artist in that organization. There is no extra pay to cover the expenses of working from home, including your insurance premiums, and you are responsible for your own health and safety.

3. Theatre Employee

If accepted as a trainee or wig-assistant in a wig department associated with a large theatre, perhaps producing classical drama, opera or musicals, you will become part of a team, monitored closely, mentored, trained and supported.

You may begin as a part-time knotter, working in-house, but will be expected to assist with the collection, cleaning, blocking and re-furbishing of wigs for shows, progressing into full-time work. After two years' experience as a full-time assistant wig and make-up artist, you may become a wig and make-up artist, responsible for daily maintenance and running of a show.

It is rare to find full-time work only as a dedicated wig maker or in-house knotter. Theatres need efficiency; their staff must be multi-skilled, willing to work flexibly.

Wig makers are expected to have trained as hairdressers and make-up artists too, able to style the wig they have made and to work on performances. Staff stay during the show to help with changes of wigs or hair or make-up and at the end of the performance to remove and store items safely. This work may be done in the wig room, a dressing room or one of the quick-change areas near the stage.

A senior wig and make-up artist will deal directly with the designer or costume supervisor to assess the needs of a new production and be responsible for organizing staff and materials to provide them within the time and budget allotted.

They will deal with the stage manager of the show to arrange fittings for the cast and attend note sessions if required after the technical and dress rehearsals. Communication within the organization and with the members of the department is the key to success.

Unlike the wig company, the theatre will expect flexible working hours, including evenings and weekends. Even if the show does not travel the country, there are usually several auditoriums to be serviced in one organization.

When a show tours, the theatre will require staff to travel with the shows. The senior wig and make-up artist will become wig mistress/master for that run of performances, running the touring wig department, reverting to senior status on return.

Seniors may be regarded as deputy heads of department and are qualified to run departments in other venues when they leave.

The wig mistress/master/head of wig department is responsible to the production manager directly or the head of costume for administering the wig staff, and supervising their work rooms, possibly in several auditoriums or other spaces, indoors and out. This involves employing, training and mentoring staff, record keeping, monitoring health and safety, planning, and distributing workloads and responsibilities.

The role ensures the production and servicing of each show achieves, adheres to or exceeds the standards of expectation set by the director and designer. These standards are overseen at every performance by the stage and company managers.

Backstage, each department is part of one diverse team: the crew. Communication, mutual support and respect are vital to ensure you are all working to the same goals and vision.

4. Freelance Wig Supplier

Designers, producers, actors, production managers and costume supervisors who have worked with you, or those who have seen your advertising, will make contact to offer work to support them when they are employed elsewhere, including on films and television.

Films and television:

- Your skills are readily transferable. Be prepared to work in different locations for each job, travelling is as predictable as knowing that each job lasts only for a limited time.
- You may be contacted by the wardrobe department, the make-up department or by the key hair directly to supply wigs or pieces and may be required to stay to fit them on the actor.

A freelance career may have begun to finance your training, or started later, after a time employed in a theatre or a wig business. After developing the confidence to work alone, you have become a sole trader, advertising for work, supplying private clients with their personal needs and making wigs, pieces and facial or body hair for theatre, film and other media work.

The personal client market can be for fashion and style or it may be that the client has a health issue, specifically hair loss whether through alopecia or chemotherapy, for example. Your wigs can make a big difference to these clients. At one point, the NHS would source wigs, but often without fittings. Now a client may be given a grant for their wig, but it will only cover the cost of a pre-bought one, styled to the client. Wigs will be bought in and adapted, or custom made, cut and styled by you, supplied ready to wear on stage or on film, online or at home. Delivery by the agreed time is crucial, as is obtaining permission to use their photos of the hair in your future advertising. Agree these terms in advance.

As you will not be caring for each item after delivery, legally you must ensure they are robust and suited for purpose. If not, your clients have several public platforms to vent their criticisms and there will be no repeat bookings.

Take a deposit to cover the cost of materials and allow your client to pay securely online or with their card so they are reassured of their consumer rights.

Send photos as often as you/they like, but always after the final styling, before receiving final payment.

Recorded or tracked delivery is expensive but vital. Make sure your packaging is smart and shows the client's address and the return address clearly.

When sending a styled wig to a client, it is good to keep supplies of tissue paper, bubble wrap and other padding for supporting the foundation inside the wig, as well as the exterior

PRO TIP
Huge wig with wide-holed foundation? Drive thin metal skewers through the whole piece until it is supported within the box like a sea urchin.

shape and style.

The variety of styles and materials requested of you is limited only by imagination, as are the methods to produce them.

QUICK REMINDER OF THE BASICS

- BECTU is the Broadcasting, Entertainment, Communications and Theatre Union. Contact them online. They will give you the recommended day rates for your work and help with contracts and insurance.
- You must have at least third-party insurance in case a product you use causes an allergic reaction for the actor.
- Keep up to date on and comply with health and safety regulations.
- You may not need an accountant at first, but you must keep clear records of any freelance pay and all outgoing expenses. If you are working from home, a proportion of your home expenses can be set against your freelance income, as well as the materials and tools you use and some travelling costs. You must declare all these at the end of the tax year.
- HMRC themselves will help you with this, online, gov.uk or contact the Citizens Advice Bureau. Advice is free and friendly from both.
- There are handy apps to download. Use one to keep track of your expenses and income from the very beginning, photo each receipt, however small the sum. The cost of starting up your own business can be considerable, especially if you are investing in equipment, lace and hair supplies. Even the smallest outgoings will mount up over the year. If recorded, these can be offset against taxable profits.

WIG DESIGNER

You will develop working relationships with several designers, who will request your work, but usually it is the head of wardrobe or the costume supervisor who will be your direct contact – you may not meet the designer.

Occasionally you will be sent a script, cast list and cast photos before seeing the designs. At this first meeting, the head of costume will show you the existing costume designs so you can see the aesthetic of the show. These designs may have no heads, or just an outline to suggest the hair or wig requirements. You will discuss alternative styles and how to achieve them on time and in budget. Be familiar with a way of showing examples for quick reference of how the actor could look. Better to air these suggestions now, rather than in front of the actor. Usually at this point they have met the cast, but you have not. Costume fittings may have begun. The designer may have already picked up on any possible areas of difficulty with the production and prepare you for the wig fitting when you will be meeting the actor for the first time.

You will find a technical solution to ensure the actor's wig is appropriate to the costume designs while allowing them to give their best performance for the director – all while keeping within the time and money available.

Make clear to the head of costume that you realize you are here to support them. A wig designer is not a diva; they are ready and willing to be an extra pair of hands. Your supervisor may have already allocated some work to other people, perhaps a resident wig person who will be able to cover most appearances out of their stock, or another freelance wig person known to an actor personally, who will be making their wig. Contact them and discuss your own input to make it clear that you are all working to the same ends and standards.

DEADLINES

A clear deadline is essential. Usually all wig work will be required for wear on stage by the technical rehearsal date, when a show is worked through slowly and in detail, before the dress rehearsal the following day. Often the deadline is much sooner because the wig is needed for publicity photographs. Or it might be an integral part of the action of the play and needed for rehearsal.

- If someone else is making a headdress or hat to be worn with the wig, they will need the wig from you earlier for fitting.
- If there are other wig staff, they will need it several days before the technical rehearsal to style it and prepare their own pre-show appointments list.

Once you have your timescale, schedule a final fitting with the actor and designer, at an appointment you will have made with the stage manager. Find that final deadline, then make your personal deadline before then to allow time for the unforeseen – accidents, illness, late delivery of supplies, alterations to the design. You should always aim to come in before the final deadline and under budget. This means you will have the time and resources to make tweaks if necessary.

This might happen because an actor has changed the colour or length of their own hair, put in or removed extensions, or occasionally the actor may have made considerable changes to their

performance during rehearsal and a rethink has been necessary regarding style, structure, length, colour or method of fitting and removing.

Sometimes it is the costume that has changed, and this impacts the wig design.

You may sense as you make the wig that changes should be made to its design or construction. It is your responsibility to share these thoughts but do bear in mind that any diversion from the original design should be double-checked with the designer beforehand.

Taking such things into consideration, you will work backwards from the earliest deadline to discover how much time remains to make the wig and deliver it. Now you will be pleased that you spent time at home building up speed!

All work should be recorded. Keep detailed notes about preparing the actor's hair, the wig design, dressing and styling methods. Copy this to the wig or wardrobe staff along with the wig itself.

Useful questions to ask:

- Is the wig hair permed?
- Is the colour temporary or permanent?
- How long was the actor's hair at fitting?
- Which adhesive is best for this wig?
- Is the hair human, animal or fibre?

The fitting, making and styling of wigs begin in Chapter 4.

PRO TIP

Keep communicating with your co-workers as you go. This will allow everyone to meet their deadlines too.

EXAMPLE THEATRICAL PRODUCTION TIMELINE

- First contact with someone from the production company.
- Meet designer/director and establish aesthetic and other details.
- Meet actor – fit for hair/make-up. Record from every angle. Add the names of the actor, the character(s) and play. Take measurements and shells.
- During making, you may have another fitting to ensure the design conforms to requirements and is comfortable.
- Final fitting with actor and designer to ensure they are happy with the outcome.
- Publicity photos.
- Rehearsals (from this point until opening night, the director may also make changes to styling or structure).
- Technical rehearsal. From now on, the wig will need maintenance, and you may be required to work the show.
- Dress rehearsal.
- Preview performances.
- Opening night. The show is set at a standard which must now be met every performance. Alterations stop for the most part, though maintenance and repair may begin. Be aware of understudy considerations.
- Regular performances. Clean/repair as needed.
- Closing night.

WIG-MAKING DUTIES

As wig maker, you may simply be making and delivering the wigs the theatre has specified after receiving a copy of the design, a shell or computer model of the actor's head and colour samples to match for the hair. A sample of natural hair colours is surprisingly expensive to buy, but you may create a little sample palette of your own to take to a fitting to ensure an accurate colour match. You will often find that blending two or three shades is the best way to do this. Often the hair at the middle and nape is darker as it has had less exposure to the sun.

Include notes to the wig staff when you deliver the wig and they will contact you if alterations become necessary as the show is mounted.

They usually expect items to be cut and styled ready for a final fitting, so be clear about this requirement in your contract.

You may be asked to stay or be available to alter and maintain the wig during the production period, until after the first night, or the first public performance, when the actor or a member of costume staff may take over the responsibility of maintenance.

If you stay, make sure the wigs and hairpieces you are responsible for are clean and dressed and in the right places for each actor for the show. This may be in the wig room if there is one, or beside the stage in a quick-change area, or in the actor's own dressing room. Be prepared to rescue, clean, restyle and return these for the next performance.

During the performances, help by putting on and removing the wigs as well as cleaning and re-dressing them between shows. Nothing gives you clearer feedback on your work, from the actor and the other staff, so always offer to do this.

Hair colour samples.

The Sixteenth Century: History, Hairstyles and Plays

2

This chapter will look at styles the designer might be considering in the context of the sixteenth century generally, and more specifically in those plays of the period you may be working on.

This period covers the reign of the Tudor monarchs, more usually remembered as the time of Henry VIII, Queen Elizabeth I, the Armada, the plague and possibly most relevant, Shakespeare.

This book divides itself by century, as (almost) do the British royal houses of Tudor and Stuart, Elizabeth Tudor having arranged for James Stuart to reign after her death which came in 1604. Shakespeare's work bridges the sixteenth and seventeenth centuries, so this book uses a range of his characters from both centuries, distinguished by either the sixteenth-century Tudor monarchy or the seventeenth-century Stuart monarchy. One century is, of course, just a continuation of the other, as seen in fashions of the time. The populace would not be able to afford or justify the purchase of a whole new dress when the old one or a hand-me-down may be cut, added to or embellished depending on fashion and requirement. The more defined moments of distinction are outlined in this chapter. For most Elizabethans, we can assume their daily concerns were finding employment for money to buy food and shelter from the weather; and how to keep out of trouble with their neighbours, the Church and the law.

During this time, the population is estimated to have doubled. In 1525, an estimated 2.26 million people lived in Britain. By 1601, that estimate had risen to 4.1 million.

As ever in Britain, the weather was the greatest concern and we cannot overestimate its impact on daily life. Scientific records of planetary activity and daily weather records were methodically kept and reveal that from 1508 to 1531, the autumns were cooler than before and preceded winters with icy easterly winds and far cooler temperatures throughout spring. Wet summers only worsened crop yields. Perhaps the prayers of the populace were answered, as the years 1540 to 1541 were known as the Great Tudor Drought. Wages shrank by half and the cost of living soared.

After 1550, the climate in Britain and Europe had cooled so significantly that, as an example, from this point on, we see continuous growth in glaciers. In the 1590s there were again exceptionally poor harvests leading to food shortages. The peak of this cooling was not to come until the next century with the coldest recorded decade, the 1690s.

To mitigate the effects of disastrous harvests, agricultural workers on low wages moved into towns, usually London, looking for employment where they were fed and housed. Those who could usually grew their own vegetables, brewed beer and kept some animals. Home was a smaller space than might be assumed from visiting surviving sixteenth-century properties. The average cottage of a husbandman (a

Shakespeare's birthplace, 1847, engraved by W. J. Linton after a drawing by Edward Duncan.

LEFT: Portrait of Princess Elizabeth Tudor painted for her father, Henry VIII, in c. 1546.

Shakespeare's birthplace interior.

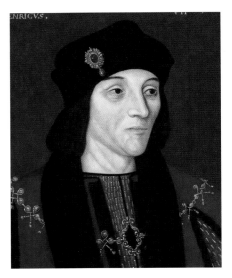

King Henry VII, by unknown artist,
National Portrait Gallery.

rural labourer) in 1500 was a one-room structure.

This home was not a warm place, merely a shelter from the biting wind. Although there was no glass in the window, there would have been wooden shutters, opened to let out the smoke if there was a fire. Even with a rushlight, it would have been dark. Unmarried people stayed with their families or shared accommodation.

A working man would have been in his twenties before he could afford marriage, unlike royals who might marry in their teens. A married couple's home might have small additions such as a cool dairy space, a laundry area, access to a well, and an outside privy. If they owned the property, a record number of people installed chimneys to heat their homes more efficiently and added glass to the windows to keep the heat in. Floors were installed beneath the roof for storage and to house truckle beds, accessed by ladder.

Shakespeare's father, John, a tradesman with six children who at one point held the equivalent position of

Mayor of Stratford-upon-Avon, needed two adjoining cottages in Henley Street to hold his family, William's young family and the glove-making workshop that sustained them.

Now let us look at the effects of all this on styles of dress and hair, starting with the A-list of the day, royalty.

STYLES OF DRESS AND HAIR

Men's Hair Fashions in Henry VIII's England

When Henry VIII became king at eighteen, he wore his hair in a chin-length bob, rather like his father. This, with a clean-shaven jaw, was the prevailing adult fashion. The style can be seen earlier in a portrait of Richard III, another of Henry VII and equally in a woodcut illustration of a farmer, in *A Newe Tracte for Husbandrye*, by John Fitzherbert, published in 1525.

Simple to maintain, the well-combed bob fits well with the ubiquitous floppy-

brimmed hats and the large collars of coats, worn indoors and out, of the time. Combs were readily available to all, from mercers in towns or pedlars in villages.

Working men with short bob and wide brimmed floppy hat or cap. This engraving from Fitzherbert's *Boke of Surveying and Improvements*, 1523.

For the farmer it only needed a cut every
six months or so with simple shears,
used equally for domestic and
agricultural purposes. A fringe was
optional, but was often a practical way
of keeping hair off the face. The clean-
shaven aspect of the farm worker
illustrated is more doubtful, and
probably artistic licence. Although facial
hair can be trimmed with shears, the
blade of an open razor, for a smooth
face, might have to be wielded by
someone else at the weekly market or
public barber shop in town and was
therefore an expense.

In 1535 King Henry VIII, according to
Stow's *Annales*, gave a command that,
'all about his court should poll their
heads'. His own hair was cut short. He
had already allowed his beard and
moustache to grow, though never to be
longer than the Adam's apple. There is a
rule in fashion that when 'everyone is
doing it' the time has come for a
change. Certainly, there is often an urge
for younger ones to put off the
conventions of their elders when
possible, but Henry was now forty-four
years old. This style had been adopted
abroad years before and Henry would
have seen King Francis with his short
hair and bearded chin at The Field of
the Cloth of Gold in June 1520. So why
did he adopt it now?

Henry VIII might have been
attempting to disguise his thickening
chin as he aged and bloated. Five years
later his waist had expanded to 52
inches (132cm). Although he was
already married to Anne Boleyn, he was
suspected of taking a new mistress.
Henry VIII demonstrated his personal

Portrait of Henry VIII with short hair and full beard – Hans Holbein the Younger, Google
Art Project.

control over everything, and decrees regarding hair meant little after he arranged the deaths of long-term colleagues and assumed control of the Church. Henry VIII believed that the money that would come from the Dissolution of the Monasteries would solve his bankruptcy, fund his policies abroad and buy loyalty.

Many men had already grown their beards with the longer bob style as convenience often trumps fashion. Monasteries had been required to employ a barber surgeon to shave the monks' tonsures, the circular crown of the head, and clean shave their beard hair. This was as much a sanitary aid as a holy requirement. Monks were forbidden to shed blood, so these same barbers with their sharp tools were trusted to carry out bloodletting, a regular treatment of the time, as well as surgery and dentistry. Physicians existed, but believed their purpose was to recognize and diagnose illnesses, perhaps offering medicine and dietary advice. Surgery was too close to animal husbandry and midwifery and considered beneath their dignity.

The Barbers Guild had been recognized for 200 years, but in 1540 they were officially renamed The Guild of Barber Surgeons. Hans Holbein painted a commemorative picture, with Henry in the middle of a group of senior members. Only six have full beards like Henry.

In wartime, barbers were an essential part of the army, treating wounds and doing amputations, alongside shaving off the lice that might infest a large group of mobile men.

Coincidentally, the closing of the monasteries put many of these men out of work. Was this Henry's job creation scheme to keep up their skills before implementing his wars?

Henry had established the armoury at Greenwich to provide the weapons of war, but the razors and shears needed by the barbers were prepared by the members of The Worshipful Company of Cutlers.

Generally, the blades were imported, and the cutlers transformed them into tools by riveting handles on to the razors and bending over the blades of shears to make the spring. There were cutlers in most towns providing knives, shears and razors for everyday use.

Scissors were imported ready-made and had been in use since Roman times for cutting cloth and hair, but were more expensive than shears and needed frequent sharpening and re-screwing. They were supplied by the mercers in several sizes and qualities.

In 1511, preparing for court revels, Richard Gibson is recorded as having bought 'of feyn sesors of breges making, xxiii payer' and 'ix payer of kolen scheres, iii tolovs scheres'. They were given heavy use as he reports that 'they were all spent and utterly worn to nothing... and sum brokyn in the revels' (from 'The Great Wardrobe Accounts' quoted in *Queen Elizabeth's Wardrobe Unlock'd* by Janet Arnold).

The new shorter hairstyle required the regular attention and skill of a professional barber; an expensive choice, open to the court, the gentry and middle classes. This was a look that was sanitary, easy to maintain with daily combing and comfortable.

It served to emphasize the increasingly bulky and wide-shouldered fashions of their clothes. The barbers also used their tools to trim the beards and moustaches. Hats were invariably worn for warmth. The portraits of Henry by Holbein and Joos van Cleve famously epitomize the look.

Women's Hair Fashion in Henry VIII's England

There was a long-standing tradition, based on biblical teaching in the letters of St Paul, that women should grow their hair but keep it covered except from their husbands.

The simplest practical solution was to wear all hair pulled back from the face, then cover it.

Henry VIII and the Barber Surgeons, by Hans Holbein the Younger, Richard Greenbury, and others.

Catherine of Aragon in gable headdress, 1530, attributed to Joannes Corvus.

Jane Seymour in gable headdress with veil tucked up to the nape, Hans Holbein.

At court, the ladies' necks were left exposed and sometimes the very front hair, with a centre parting, is seen under the expensively trimmed, English gable-hooded headdresses with long veils at the back.

Sometimes these veils were folded forward and pinned on the top of the headdress, to expose the nape. Jane Seymour often wore hers in this way, as in the Holbein portrait of 1536. In church, the veil was let down and brought forward, hiding face and hair. Shadows or scarves and veils were also used outdoors for travelling or hunting,

to cover the entire face from the cold wind and protect from the tanning effect of the sun.

Long hair was brushed or combed frequently. The hair, parted in the middle, was plaited tightly on each side using a single three-yard ribbon or lace, long enough to reach the end of the plait and still leave a foot-length loose for tying.

After both sides had been plaited and tied off, they were lifted and crossed over the head, just behind the ear-to-ear line. The ribbon dangling from each end was then threaded through a blunt

needle, called a bodkin, and used to bind the plaits together and to the under hair.

When this hairstyle was worn under a cap or a hood, a pair of sharp pins pushed through the material could secure the headdress into the plaits. The historian Janet Arnold, author of *Queen Elizabeth's Wardrobe Unlock'd* has demonstrated how the hair plaiting and lacing was actually a fast and simple way of styling the hair that could be done by a woman without a maid to help or even a mirror.

Outside the court, female fashion

remained strictly practical. Washing the hair was considered dangerous and unhealthy; lye soap irritated the skin and was painful in the eyes. Washing was believed to remove too much of the natural oils and without conditioner, combing out of long hair was a painful process. Sitting by the fire to dry the hair was believed to risk your health by catching cold. Instead, as a dry shampoo, powdered corn meal was used

to absorb the grease and then the hair thoroughly combed. The comb moved the powder and natural oils down the hair, collecting dust and debris as it went. The comb itself could be safely

washed. Keeping hair hidden also concealed the smell.

A positive outcome of the regular combing with fine teeth was to lessen the risk of head lice or at least to keep their numbers down. Although many recipes for their elimination existed, mostly based on dung and ash, the only sure way to be rid of them remained the shaving of the head. A hair covering limited opportunities for head lice to infest a clean head and hid a shaven one.

Wealthy young and unmarried women might wear their hair loose and uncovered, for a social event.

It was more practical in most households for women to wear their hair off the face, pulled into plaits with lacing and covered with a linen cap held with a pin. The cap could be washed. Caps were worn outdoors under the hat for warmth.

Poorer women continued to wrap their hair in a cloth to keep it off the face and hidden. A two-metre length of linen, approximately 75cm wide, was wrapped over the forehead and covered the ears. The ends could be knotted at the nape and brought forward around the neck like a scarf or cravat.

This cloth, like the veils or shadows of the wealthy, when wrapped high around or over the chin and even covering the mouth was protection from the cold, dust and bad smells associated with ill health. Sometimes, the ends of cloth might be taken to the top of the head and knotted or pinned flat, or simply taken back to the nape, tied off and left. A hat was worn over the wrapped cloth. The hair underneath could be pulled into a single twisted tail and held in a bun with a sharp wooden or bone pin, or the hair might be plaited and tied off, hanging in a tail at the nape. For a special event, the wrap was bleached, starched and the folds more carefully arranged.

Saskia van Uylenburgh in Arcadian costume by Rembrandt.

French hood showing the hair at the front. Portrait of Anne Boleyn, by an unknown artist.

At court, from the 1530s the linen cap might be replaced with a satin one, and pearls or embroidery added. It was worn further back on the head, still showing the centre parting. This allowed the front hair to be swept down over the ears on either side to soften the look. The English gable-angled headdress was often replaced with the French hood style, almost a jewelled Alice band over the ears, with the obligatory veil at the back. Headdresses held wires inside the front, which could be bent tightly to the head for security as well as supporting the style. The veil was pinned into the hair as usual, but these are sharp copper alloy or brass pins, not hairpins. The first metal hairpins were not recorded until 1545; before that, wood, shell and bone pins were available for holding hair, but were unsuitable for pinning through cloth.

Fashion in Elizabeth I's England

Neither the reign of Mary I, the brief arrival of Lady Jane Grey, or Edward VI affected fashion noticeably, but when Elizabeth took the throne in 1558, aged twenty-five, a change became evident. The younger men at court grew their hair longer, but always to sit above the fashionable ruff which so snugly kept out the draught, while reflecting light back up to the face, refreshing tired expression lines.

A broad and high brow was considered attractive in both sexes, so hair was generally brushed up off the face. Beards and moustaches became more stylish and well groomed, sometimes both hair and beard being 'crisp'd', that is, curled with heated irons.

Hats and caps remained a constant feature for men. These caps were often highly decorated and embroidered, but simply styled like those they wore for bed.

François van Valois by Emanuel van Meteren.

Older men might wear a hat that looked like the usual flat cap of Henry's day but with an extension down over the ears to cover the nape hair above the ruff.

For women, the change was more dramatic. Etiquette was to follow the Queen's lead in matters of fashion. As an unmarried woman and as a marriageable commodity, Elizabeth could show her hair, but as the monarch, she needed gravitas, a neat head shape. The compromise was to wear just a few curls, loose but prominent on her shoulders, and the rest of her hair controlled in a laced and plaited bun, on or just below the crown of her head. The jewelled French hood, now worn behind the ears, revealed as much hair as possible while retaining at the back a veil covering the bun.

Alternatively, without loose curls at her neck and with the laced and plaited hair at the back covered with a jewelled hairnet called a caul, she could present herself more severely. Two of these cauls, one knitted in gold thread, the other in silver, were given to her as New Year's presents in the winter of 1561. The caul worked easily under the perkier hats that came to replace the soft berets during the 1560s and were frequently worn indoors as well as out.

To soften that look, but with no sense of a loss of control, she wore her hair fuller by curling the front hair. In 1564 Sir James Melville, the Scottish emissary, described her hair as being 'more reddish than yellow and curled in appearance naturally'. There are early references in 'The Great Wardrobe Accounts' to the purchase of said curled hair. Roger Montague, the Queen's silk

Elizabeth with loose curls on shoulders in the Rainbow Portrait, 1570, by Nicholas Hilliard.

Elizabeth with hair styled up in the Pelican Portrait, 1573, by Nicholas Hilliard.

man supplied whole 'heads' of curled or rolled hair. It was safer and less painful to pin these ready-made curls over her own hair, rather than undergoing hot tonging. Even in skilled hands, the process of heating the irons in the fire and testing the temperature on a slip of paper or cloth, or even by spitting on them, risked burning the royal head. These extra curls, once purchased, would last well. They could be refreshed by washing, wrapping up in wooden rollers, tying and boiling them, then leaving to dry. A time-consuming chore

when a simple answer is, if you have the money, to buy more curls.

The fuller hairstyle was emulated at court by ladies padding out or rolling up their hair on either side of the centre parting, with some investing in extra curls like Elizabeth. The back hair

remained plaited and laced in a jewelled net or caul. The whole framed by a huge ruff or standing collar of starched lace. Roger Montague supplied these ready-made pads of hair too.

The inevitable next step for a busy working queen was to save time by buying complete wigs – expensive, but able to be worn like hats, providing warmth and instant, pain-free style. Roger Montague provided these wigs too, sending 'two periwigs of haire' in 1592 and again four 'perewigges of heaire' in 1595, six in 1601 and six more

NOTES

The Third Tudor Woman's wig in Chapter 5 is a short, curled up-do for a queen.

in 1602. He supplied fine nets made of human hair, sometimes studded with pearls, or other beads, for instant decoration.

The wig was something else the ladies of court could and did copy. Even the older, married women would now display their hair in court, and they also appreciated the convenience and warmth of a wig.

Elizabeth's wigs had another use, as portrait painters could work from the wig along with the Queen's clothes, perhaps arranged on a lady-in-waiting or a padded dummy, to spare the Queen the boredom of sitting more than a few times for a likeness. This would explain the unusual angle of a wig or crown in some of her portraits.

Extravagant hairstyles might suit for a court ball or banquet or attending a masque, but another smart, comfortable and socially acceptable look was to wear the coiffe, a development of the simple linen cap, but lace-edged and embroidered, worn alone or under a hat, to hide the hair and keep the ears warm. This item could become as extravagantly embellished as the owner could afford, and again, there are references to them as New Year gifts to the Queen. All women wore something similar, but plainer, at night. These styles remained fashionable until the end of the century, when at court we see higher, beehive hairstyles displayed by ladies and longer hair with lovelocks, and small pointed beards and moustaches on some gentlemen.

WIGS IN PERFORMANCE

Theatrical Wig Dressing for Sixteenth-Century Plays

Now that we have refreshed our overview of hairstyles in the sixteenth century, we can look at some of the occasions when the playwright has set us the challenge of reproducing the look on stage. There are of course many surviving plays from Shakespeare's contemporaries (Christopher Marlowe, Ben Johnson, Thomas Kyd, John Fletcher, John Marston and so on) or it may be a modern writer using the historical setting, but for ease of reference we have used Shakespeare's more popular characters.

In sixteenth-century plays you may well need to show courtly hairstyles for Elizabethan men and women, but there are plenty of other scenes which cover the full extent of life, death (natural or unnatural), health and sickness (real and feigned), for soldiers and civilians, urban and rural. Additionally, there are mythological and magical fantasy characters of his knowledge and imagination. Enough to keep one busy for a lifetime.

Plays are not a history lesson, but entertainment. A dramatic experience or a look that makes clear the story of the play and character, rather than a pedantic recreation of famous portraits. Presentation may be more important to the director or designer. Performance is not always re-enactment.

Knowledge of period styles does not entitle you to dispute this. On the other hand, you are not bound by the methods of any historical period to achieve your results. This book aims to show that modern materials and safe practices bring success.

Character, Action and Wigs in Plays

Other problems you will encounter are those thrown up by the journey through the play of your character. Benedick in *Much Ado About Nothing* removes his beard part way through the play. The lovers in *A Midsummer Night's Dream* run away to the woods in the night, getting muddy and bedraggled before the next day attending a court wedding party. Characters may become ill and die like King Henry IV; go mad and get soaked in a thunderstorm like King Lear; be involved in bloody fights (too many to mention); or dancing and climbing to a balcony like Romeo; strip naked and cover themselves in mud to seem mad, like Edgar in *King Lear*.

Other difficulties to face are reaching an actor to change their appearance before them descending through the air like Ariel or the goddesses in *The Tempest* or Jupiter in *Cymbeline* or rising through a trapdoor. The actor playing Caliban in *The Tempest* hides by crawling under a gabardine (waterproof coat) in another thunderstorm and will need extra-firm wig fixing.

You will notice how important the weather and travelling outdoors are in these plays, as it was ever present in the lives of the writer and theatre patrons. Drama delights in surprising the audience. Be ready to be surprised with wind and rain, ice and snow on stage, not always digitally enhanced.

Whatever the problem, your director has probably already made a choice and you will provide the means to achieve that end.

NOTES

These techniques are covered in Chapters 4, 5 and 6.

Frontispiece to *The Wits* (1662), showing theatrical drolls, attrib. Francis Kirkman – *The Wits, or, Sport upon Sport* frontispiece.

Gender Swaps

Women are well represented in plays written in the sixteenth and seventeenth centuries, but when we know that in public these parts were performed by boys, that may seem surprising. However, that very contradiction gives dramatic irony to an audience who enjoy knowing more than the characters on stage. On numerous occasions, cross-dressing supplies the humour or supports the intrigues of plot. This tradition continued even when women moved onto the public stage. The male impersonators of music hall and the drag kings of today, the panto dames and the drag queens, all give a conspiratorial nod to their audiences who feel welcomed into the pretence. Disguises give female characters more freedom and allow Shakespeare to play with gender norms. For example, Rosalind in *As You Like It,* disguised as a youth to escape a repressive regime; Portia and Nerissa in *The Merchant of Venice*, disguised as a lawyer and his clerk; Viola, in *Twelfth Night*, shipwrecked on a beach in a foreign land, then disguised as her own brother; Julia in *Two Gentlemen of Verona* disguised as a page to follow her beloved Proteus to Milan; Imogen in *Cymbeline* disguised as a page to travel to Wales. The Third Tudor Man's wig in Chapter 4 guides you through creating this style of wig.

The rich spectrum of gender diversity and fashion supplies directors and designers with cast who do not always need cross-dressing wigs to carry the plot of the play forward if the element of disguise is already clear. Re-gendering the casting of ballets, musicals, plays and films has provided fresh insights to cultural norms and can point to unacknowledged gender biases. An actor with longer hair, worn up and styled as a woman, may find no wig is needed, just the style changed. They may for instance be simply styled as a boy by hair being let down and tied back at the nape.

But if this character is supposed to have cut her own hair, as in Joan of Arc's situation, the 'boy' wig should look completely convincing.

In *Twelfth Night*, Viola may need to begin in a straggled, wet-look wig as she is rescued from the sea (*see* the First Stuart Man in Chapter 7 for styling techniques) and Rosalind in *As You Like It* may need a more formal court wig in the opening scenes (*see* Chapter 5: the First Stuart Woman). There will be quick changes out of these and Shakespeare, an actor himself, can be relied on to allow scripted time for the wig and costume change out of girl, into boy, generally providing between fifty and eighty lines of dialogue, according to the Professor of Shakespeare and Renaissance Literature at the University of Warwick, Jonathan Bate CBE.

If the actor's own hair is not right for the short look as 'male' before the show, you can do a secure preparation that will be suitable for the masculine style of wig to also cover. This can be any preparation that keeps the natural head shape.

Sometimes, it is the need to establish that we are dealing with twins that makes the provision of wigs useful. The sixteenth century, with religiously endorsed differences in hair length between male and female fashions, gave Shakespeare a binary gender shorthand for disguising his female characters. Ben Jonson also used this in *Epicene, or The Silent Woman* written in 1609, where a boy is disguised with a long wig and offered up as a bride. *Volpone,* premiered at the Globe in 1606, features the character of Androgyne, a hermaphrodite. Younger women adopted a flatter hairstyle instead of the high oval beehive with ringlets to the shoulder. Young men, clean shaven and longer haired than before, looked similar.

Apart from the need in some plays for a disguise to further the plot, designers use hair colour and style similarities for twins, such as the two sets in *The Comedy of Errors*. Family members for instance in the history plays may also be coloured similarly to help the audience keep track of who is whom.

In addition, there is the ever-present question of finance. A wig is cheaper to provide than an extra cast member, so doubling-up (or more!) of roles by putting the actor in a wig is as common in productions of Shakespeare's plays today as it was in Shakespeare's day.

Preparing for Wig and Facial Hair Making

3

This chapter gives detailed directions for setting up your wig room, fittings, preparing the actor's hair, measuring the actor's head and taking a shell. See Chapter 4 for making foundations and knotting the male Tudor looks.

SETTING UP A WORKROOM AT HOME – SPACE AND TOOLS REQUIRED

If you are freelance, or knotting at home, allocate a space as the wig room. This will save a lot of worry and burnt-out vacuum cleaners later.

Wig Room Essentials

- A window to clear the air after using chemicals and to give good light for checking hair colours, access to a sink for cleaning wigs and no carpet.
- The door should close if you share your home with children or animals.
- The table should be at least 70cm square, so you can lay your lace flat for cutting out.

PRO TIP

The most expensive single item will be your wig stand. It is not just for wig dressing, many people prefer to whip and knot on their stand, buy the best you can afford. Second-hand items, as with all wig-making kit, are worth searching for. A good-quality stand will last a lifetime.

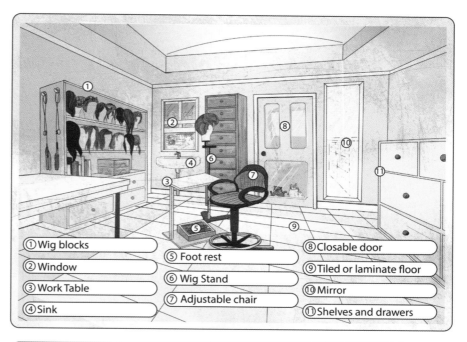

① Wig blocks	⑤ Foot rest	⑧ Closable door
② Window	⑥ Wig Stand	⑨ Tiled or laminate floor
③ Work Table	⑦ Adjustable chair	⑩ Mirror
④ Sink		⑪ Shelves and drawers

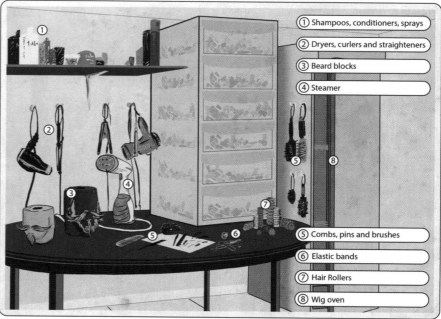

| ① Shampoos, conditioners, sprays |
| ② Dryers, curlers and straighteners |
| ③ Beard blocks |
| ④ Steamer |
| ⑤ Combs, pins and brushes |
| ⑥ Elastic bands |
| ⑦ Hair Rollers |
| ⑧ Wig oven |

Your wig room essentials.

LEFT: Wig Room.

- Shelves and drawers for your tools and hair and lace supplies.
- Wig blocks in different sizes or ready to pad for preparation, creation, styling and display of wigs.
- An adjustable chair with footrest and back support.
- Wig stand.

Later Additions

- A hood hairdryer or a wig oven for dressing and styling wigs.
- Rollers of different sizes.
- A chin block for making beards.
- A steamer for fibre wigs.
- Wide variety of combs and brushes, hairpins and hair grips.
- Several sizes of covered elastic bands for hair.
- An assortment of curling and straightening tongs, hairdryer.
- Sprays and gels, shampoo and conditioner.

WIG-MAKING TOOLS AND EQUIPMENT

- Knotting hooks and handles.
- Cradle.
- Canvas wig blocks.
- Loose padding.
- Sticky tape.
- Parcel tape.
- Small and large pins (these are slightly thicker than dress-making

Knotting station.

pins and have larger heads).
- Contrasting colour paper to lay under the wig lace.
- Flexible tape measure.
- Small sewing scissors.
- Large scissors to cut the wig lace.
- Galloon or ribbon for blocking and micropore tape.
- Wire mats to hold the hair.
- Tailor's chalk.
- Cling film, polythene bag or open foundations.
- Lined note paper for moustache making.
- Small hammer and pliers.
- Wig laces of 15 and 20 denier nylon and 20 and 30 denier Terylene in several shades.
- Invisible nylon thread, light and dark.
- Cotton thread in bright colours.
- Needles, various sizes (curved are best).
- A doofer – a thin piece of coloured card or stiff paper, to push up under your knotting or whipping.
- A thin metal spatula or tail comb to unfurl seams.
- An angled table lamp, or even one containing a magnifying area.

WIG BLOCKS

There are polystyrene, wooden and rubber blocks and several grades of cork-filled soft blocks. You can never have too many. To begin, choose the best cork-filled soft blocks that you can afford. They are suitable for making and styling your wigs. You will need several sizes, but you can order the right size as soon as you have done a fitting, or pad the one you have with tissue and tape.

Block Types

- Glass and the red plastic ones are for making bald caps.

Blocks: Back row L–R: Long necked soft, red plastic, yellow silicone. Front row L–R: Soft cork or sawdust filled block, chin block, polystyrene head.

PRO TIP

- Use different types of knotting hook handles, each one set up ready to work with a different size hook, large, medium and small, or use the style of handle you prefer but use coloured nail varnish to differentiate them.
- **Warning:** The wooden blocks look lovely but will break your toes if you drop one and you will need extra tools to work with. Feel free to eschew entirely.

- Heavy yellow silicone ones can be used to make bald caps and wig foundations, they come in a range of larger sizes.
- Long-necked felt-covered ones are to display wigs only.
- A polystyrene block has no weight and will not sit still for you to work on it, but they are cheap, readily available and come in small sizes and different shapes. Choose one with a hole underneath to fit on your wig

stand. As with all practical crafts, prepare to make adjustments to suit you. For example, you may find the smallest size has a V-shaped neck that makes knotting awkward and will need modifying for wig making. The slightly larger 54cm one has a lip around the neck, which may need carving off before foundation making or knotting.

If, in a pinch, you need to make a foundation or knot on one, cut off the excess protrusions at the neck and cover the block in cling film and sticky tape first. Cut a horizontal groove round the neck 2cm up and another around the forehead. Tie a string around each of these, which can sit inside the groove and loop under your knotting cradle. This will secure the block while you work.

- Long-necked cork-filled blocks are useful for wig dressing, but awkward for knotting.

Check the temperature of the room for comfort and have a drink of water within reach.

THE FIRST FITTING

A Checklist to Prepare for Meeting the Actor

1. When and where: How long will you have to do the fitting? Is there a surface for your tools, chairs, mirror, enough light, enough space/air, is it quiet enough? Do you have WiFi or will you need to download and/or print out a range of reference pics?
2. Tools for preparing hair to go under a shell: Combs, hairbrush, portable curling tongs, gel, small- and medium-size elastic bands, hairpins and hair grips, clip combs, silicone bands, wig caps, tape measure,

mirror.
3. Design for wig, cast and production notes: Show and discuss using hair colour swatches, real and synthetic, front lace colour samples and pictures to bring the ideas to life.
4. Tools for taking a shell: Clear plastic bag or hairdresser's semi-circular polythene cap to make the transparent shell and tape with dispenser, various colours of marker pens to mark on the true hairline and required hairline, actor's name and info, bald patches, hair growth direction and so on. (Or several open foundations, pins and eyebrow pencils.) Scissors – hairdressing and non-hairdressing, measuring tape, measurement sheet and pen.
5. PPE: Hand sanitizer, mask and apron, wet wipes, disinfectant spray tissues, paper towel.
6. Recording: Phone or tablet, notepad and pen, camera.
7. Various options for securing the wig: Based on how active the performance is and if, or how often and how quickly, it will be removed or replaced. Use of glues/comb and pins/elastic under chin or around ears, silicone bands, wig cap options.

HOW TO PREPARE HAIR UNDER A WIG

There are plenty of different ways to prepare hair under the wig cap before taking the shell. You might use just one or a combination of the following techniques:
- Wrapping the hair.
- Braids.
- Pin curls.
- Corn rows.
- French plaits.
- Grips and/or small clip combs.

PRO TIP

- The principle is always to preserve a natural head shape.

- If the actor has long hair to conceal under the wig, you will need to protect it, especially at the ends, and especially for delicate hair such as 4C curly natural hair, hair damaged from bleach or processing, extensions and permed hair.

Discover if the wig and wig cap are to come off in a quick change, releasing the hair or does the wig cap stay on, ready for a different wig? Your actor will probably be happy to talk all about it! Consider the length of the actor's own hair and the style of wig to go over, keeping to the actor's own head shape.

There are occasions when a wig is needed over locs, extensions or extra long or thick hair, and the answer here is to hold it all securely at the nape. Divide and tie the hank into several smaller tresses to spread the thickness across the nape. You may even find you can let their hair fall down the back, inside the costume. This impacts the design of the costume equally as much as the wig so needs flagging up early. A wig cap may still be worn over the top of the head as usual, under the wig, but needs careful fixing.

If it fits with the design, a gap in the top of the wig could allow the actor's own hair to protrude and be incorporated with the wig hair, for instance as a bun or ponytail.

A second style might need to be prepared under the wig, for instance if a bun on top of the head will be revealed when the wig is removed. A clip-on bun would be one solution, but in this instance an extension in the foundation could accommodate it if the shape can be incorporated in the wig design. For example, the oval beehive of the early seventeenth century could hide an extended section of wig to hold long hair.

Wrapping the Hair

If the hair is going inside the wig, then the wrap is one solution. This is the most challenging preparation.

TOOLS:
- A good hairbrush.
- A large toothed comb.
- Tail comb.
- Hair grips.
- Wig cap.
- Hairpins.
- Water spray.
- Clip combs.

To wrap the hair, keep the top layer of prep smooth, but there will be a pin curl as base and Kirby grips and clips are needed to hold the hair securely under the wig cap.

To retain the wig cap over smoothly wrapped hair, you will need clip combs. If the hair is to be released from the wig cap and seen on stage, it will probably be wrapped for a smooth style or pin curled for a curly, fuller style. Bulky prep risks the credibility of the wig.

PRO TIP
- Practise doing this wrap on your friends to develop speed and skill. Then practise putting one wig on top of another. Remember this is added heat and discomfort for your volunteer and actor alike.
- At this stage you may spray the hair lightly with leave-in conditioner, a shine spray or just water to reduce static and make the hair easier to handle. Do not make it wet.

METHODS OF WRAPPING HAIR

Long curly hair, hair with extensions in and 4C curly hair should all be handled as little as possible to avoid damage. Section the hair gently, without trying to comb or brush through unless you are very practised and certain it won't be damaged.

Long, straight European or Asian type hair is less vulnerable, unless bleached or permed.

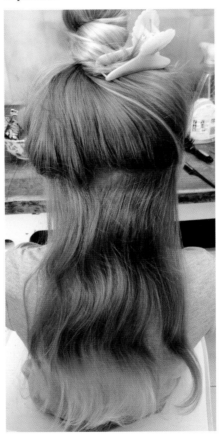

Step 1: Long, straight European hair, ready to be wrapped.

The wrap is more difficult if the hair is layered and you will use a combination of wrap and pin curls.

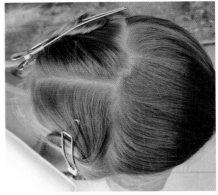

Step 2: Parted and front sectioned off.

Step 3: Front clipped out of the way.

Step 4: Crown in large, flat pin curl.

1. If necessary, before sectioning, brush through the actor's own hair to remove tangles, then use a large comb, followed with an anti-static wet wipe or dryer sheet, to draw through and knock the air out, making it more manageable.
2. Check if the wig will have a parting and copy this in the actor's own hair.
3. Separate the hair so that there is a section in front of each ear, bounded by the parting and clip it out of the way.
4. Separate a section of hair surrounding the crown and make it into a large, flat pin curl, held with two hairgrips. Bend them slightly more into an arc to mimic the head shape. Check that the top of the head still looks flat at each stage of the process.
5a. If the hair is thick or layered, separate the back hair in half horizontally by parting it level with the top of the ears, halve the top section diagonally and take one side, pull firmly up and across to the opposite side and wrap it round the pin curl and grip it.
5b. Do the same with the other side.
6. If nape hair is long enough, do the same; separate, lift and cross over, to pin around the previous pin curl. Otherwise make two or three smaller pin curls at the nape.

Step 5a: Wrap the hair around, diagonally.

Step 8a: One side of the front wrapped around and pinned.

Step 5b: Do the same with the other side.

Step 8b: The other side of the front wrapped and pinned.

Steps 6 & 7: Wrap the nape in the same way with long hair.

Step 9: Checking overall head shape.

Step 10: Toupee grips in place.

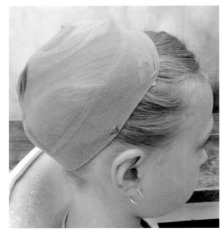

Step 11: Wig cap on behind the actor's parting.

7. If the nape hair is not too thick or layered, make just one diagonal parting from top right to bottom left with the back hair. Then take the bottom left section and pull it firmly up, across to the right, lay the hair around the pin curl and grip. Take the right side of the nape section and pull it firmly up to the left, around the pin curl and grip.

8a. Take one side of the front hair back towards the crown, in one section, wrap it round the other hair and grip.

8b. Repeat on the other side of the front.

9. Check the overall shape is smooth and looks close to a natural shape. Check the hairline all round is clear of long hairs; spray if needed to keep them back.

10. If you've made pin curls, these can now be used for anchors. If not, put small toupee clip combs into the hair above the ears and either side of the nape and parting. Set them at least a finger width in from the hairline.

11. You are now ready for the wig cap.

Braiding

Braids are useful ways to control long, bulky hair that may deform a wig style. This method keeps the top and sides of the head flat and moves the bulk to the back of the head.

TOOLS:
- A good hairbrush.
- A large toothed comb.
- Wet wipe or tumble dryer sheet.
- Tail comb.
- Sectioning clips.
- Small and large elastic bands.
- Wig cap.
- Hair grips.
- Water spray.

METHOD:
1. Brush the hair, then comb with a large toothed comb and brush over with a wet wipe, or tumble dryer sheet, to knock out the air and reduce static.
2. Use sectioning clips to separate the hair into four manageable parts.
3. Plait each side of the nape separately, pulling the hair up and

PRO TIP

- If the hair here is too short to reach the crown swirl, put it in a flat pin curl each side.
- Braiding is best for when the actor has long hair under a wig with a centre parting.
- Just cut these rubber bands off afterwards as pulling is painful and damaging.

across diagonally towards the opposite ear. Use a small elastic band at the end of each plait and hold it with a section clip.

4. Pull the first plait up towards, and level with, the opposite ear, but 5cm in from the hairline behind the ear. Make it into a large, flat pin curl over the base of the other nape plait.

5. Grip this down and repeat with the other half of the nape hair. The fullness is now over the occipital bone.

6. Make a parting to suit the wig style, and plait each side separately, pulling the hair up from the ears and back from the front. Secure the ends with small elastic bands and hold the plaits with section clips.

7. Take one of the plaits and drape it behind the nearest ear, between the hairline and nape plait, down and across the nape, above the hairline and beneath the occipital bone and grip in the end.

Repeat with the other half of the front hair, taking it down under the occipital bone, but above the nape hairline and gripping it.

Steps 1-3: Braided from the nape, up and across diagonally and clipped.

Step 4: Pin curl one plait over the base of the other.

Steps 5-7: Wrap the front plaits around the occipital bone, grip and check shape.

Corn Rows or French Plaits

These will keep the top of the head and the sides flat. The bulk will be at the back of the head by the occipital bone.

> **PRO TIP**
>
> French plaits are useful when the actor has long but layered hair under a wig with a centre parting.

Steps 1-3: French braid, elastic and finish with standard plait on both sides.

Step 4: Cross plaits and pin curl under the occipital bone, grip.

TOOLS:
- A large toothed comb.
- Wet wipe or tumble dryer sheet.
- Elastic bands in different sizes.
- Tail comb.
- Hair grips.
- Wig cap.
- Water spray.
- Hair spray.
- Clip combs.

METHOD:
1. Brush through the hair, then use a large comb and wipe to take out the air and static.
2. Start braiding from one side of the parting, at an angle towards the top of the ear, taking small sections of hair one at a time from the hairline and the parting, working as close to the roots as possible. Your fingernails should be taking the hair directly from the scalp with each twist. Keep at least 5cm in from the hairline all round to avoid damaging fine hairs on the hairline and the braids being visible.
3. Just before reaching the centre nape, put an elastic band on the hair, then finish the ends with a simple plait. Repeat this braiding with the other side of the head.
4. Cross the plaits under the occipital bone and make a pin curl behind each ear with the ends and grip them in.

Pin Curls

TOOLS:
- A brush.
- A large toothed comb.
- Tail comb.
- Hair grips.
- Wig cap.
- Hairpins.
- Water spray or with a little conditioner mixed in.
- Clip combs.

Steps 1-3a: Start at the front, pulling a section back, twisting the ends under and pinning.

Step 3b: Tuck the end of the curl under. Grip away from hairline.

Step 4: Pin curled all over.

METHOD:

1. Brush through the hair, then comb with a large toothed comb.
2. If the hair is very thick or curly, spray lightly with water with a little conditioner mixed in and comb through again. Do not make the hair wet.
3. Begin on the top of the head, at the front hairline by the parting or break if there is one. Pull a section of the hair back from the parting and crown as flat as you can and, with a twist, turn the ends under the root hair lengths at the outside edge of that section. This will make a pin curl where the ends are partially held in place by those roots.

   Depending on the thickness of the curl you can hold it with one or two hairgrips. Do not overlap or cross them. Point the ends of the grips away from the hairline so as not to catch on the wig or come loose.
4. Continue over the head till all hair is pin curled.

Grips and Clips

When hair is too short to pin curl, grip it or spray the front hair back from the hairline and position toupee clips either side of the nape and front, under the wig cap.

An alternative is to use a silicone grip bandage around the head.

PRO TIP

A balding actor is better secured with a silicone grip bandage than a wig cap, if the wig allows.

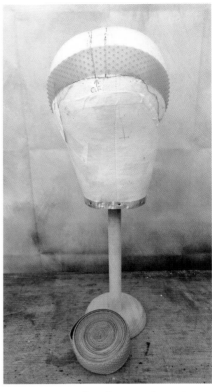

A silicone grip bandage, ready-made or buy in bulk and sew to size.

Putting on a Wig Cap

There are several reasons to use a wig cap:

- It provides a washable lining for the wig, absorbing sweat and grease.
- It controls the actor's hair, condensing it, holding it away from the hairline and supporting the hair prep.
- If there is a big difference between the wig colour and the actor's hair it will blur or hide this.
- A flesh-coloured cap can provide the illusion of a parting or thinning hair.
- The cap can be adapted to hold a mic pack.
- A securely fixed cap provides a firm base for the wig, often eliminating the need for much glue.

Various wig caps are available.

Your actor can hold the cap securely on their own forehead.

TOOLS:

- Short hairpins.
- A tail comb.
- Various coloured wig caps. Check that you have options in appropriate colours for your actor and/or wig. Flesh colour, the nearest match to the actor's own, is usually the best choice. If the wig is thin or the actor's own hair remains visible (black hair under a white wig, for example) then look for a near match to the wig hair colour.
- Different sizes of wig caps. Some wig caps are small; some types are more spacious. Make sure your actor is comfortable but that it is tight enough to support the wig.

Tuck the hair under all around with your tail comb.

METHOD:

1. Hold the cap open with both hands and stand behind the actor. Lay the front of the cap on the forehead just above the eyebrows, checking the edge is smooth and has not rolled up or under.
2. Lower the sides and back to cover the hairline all round. Check for escaping hairs around the edge of the cap with your tail comb.
3. Slide the front up on to the hairline then take it back a little more to sit over a finger width, 2cm behind the hairline.

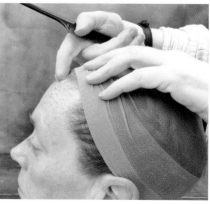
Pull the cap back from front hairline by a finger's width.

PRO TIP

- There may need to be two or more different coloured caps to accommodate successive wig changes during the performance – the second wig cap goes under the first.

- Be careful of their make-up! Made-up eyebrows and foreheads may smudge.

Open-Topped Wig Caps

If the actor's hair is thick, but not needing pin curls, you can use an open-topped wig cap following the instructions above. Distribute the top hair evenly with your tail comb once it has been pulled through the top.

SECURING THE WIG CAP

1. Use the shortest hairpins to take tiny tucks. These will hold the cap to the hair.
2. Push the pin into the cap, pointing towards the face, feel for the scalp, gently, then slide the pin away from the face and back up towards the crown.
3. Do this at intervals all around the edge of the cap.

Step 1: Secure with pins at the front first. Push the pin through the cap and towards the hairline.

Step 2: Flip the pin, gently scraping the scalp and moving back from the hairline towards the crown.

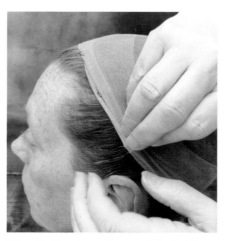

Step 3: Continue all around the hairline.

MEASURING THE HEAD FOR A WIG

Look in Appendix 2 for a printable wig measurement form.

TOOLS:
- Tape measure.
- Measurement form or the six directions in mind.
- Recording equipment.

METHOD:
1. Circumference (C) – Hold measuring tape horizontally on the front hairline and loop around the widest part of the skull, the occipital bone, making sure it lies flat and sits down behind the ears on each side. Meet tape at front and take measurement.
2. Front to nape (FN) – Hold tape vertically at front of hairline and lay over the wig cap or hair to the nape. Lay flat and take measurement.
3. Temple to temple (TT) – Hold the tape horizontally at the temple and loop around the back of the head to the other temple. Ensure it lies flat and take the measurement.
4. Ear to ear (EE) – Hold the tape vertically starting behind one ear, lie it flat over the head like a pair of headphones, take the measurement from behind the other ear.
5. Ear to nape (EN) – Hold tape diagonally from behind the top of the ear to its closest nape. Measure.
6. Across nape (AN) – Hold tape horizontally and measure across the lowest point at the bottom of the nape hairline.

Record these along with your notes from the fitting.

METHODS TO MAKE, LABEL, KEY, SPLIT AND REMOVE A SHELL

Step by step, how to make and remove a shell and restore your actor's hair.

Shells on blocks and in storage with their character/measurement notes.

Making a Shell

A shell is a 3D shape of the actor's head. Here are three methods you can use, depending on your available equipment and preference. Make sure you have practised in advance!

For all the methods, begin as so:

1. Explain to the actor exactly what you plan to do and why. Wear a face mask and an apron.
2. Prep the actor exactly as for the wig, with their own hair parted, distributed and fixed, plaited, wrapped, gripped or gelled back from hairline, under a wig cap or silicone bandage.
3. Keep a record of the hair prep that you have done under the wig cap.
4. Measure the actor's head and fill in the measurement sheet (*see* Appendix 2).

The Open Foundation

TOOLS:
- Several open foundations.
- Pins.
- Scissors.
- Marker pen.

A range of open foundations in different sizes.

- Sticky tape.

An open foundation is a two- or three-piece foundation, using strong net instead of a front lace, only a single whipping line to hold the sections together and without an outside hem at the nape.

METHOD:

1. Put on the foundation as for a wig. If tight, the front seam whipping is easily opened with scissors and re-set with pins. Use the small strong blocking pins. Dressmaking pins tend to slip out.
2. Tuck the nape with pins to fit. Point pins at the very bottom of the nape upwards.

3. Add the hairline, eyebrows, parting, hair growth direction, actor's name and other notes with an eyebrow pencil if you want to re-use, or a marker pen if you don't.
4. Instead of cutting a key, mark each side of a seam or tuck with your marker pen, then you can take out the pins to ease the shell off. This item, although still made with a synthetic fibre, can be cleaned and re-used, unlike the plastic shells below.

Plastic Wrap Shells

Shells sent as part of a commission are usually made like the plastic ones detailed here to be only for that actor or client. You can keep them stored alphabetically by actor's name. Cling film is trickier to use because it sticks to itself. If you choose to use this method, go heavy on the sticky tape on the inside of the shell too.

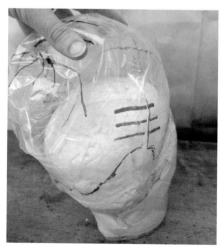

A plastic shell coming smoothly off the block.

CLING FILM SHELL

TOOLS:
- Cling film in a dispenser.
- A roll of sticky tape in a dispenser or clear parcel tape, and a spare roll.
- Permanent marker pens in at least two colours: one for marking the hairline, another for the actor's name and notes, and alterations to the hairline. These can be in any colour that will show against their skin and hair.
- Scissors, small and sharp, not hairdressing.

METHOD:
1. Take a sheet of cling film and wrap it firmly at an angle around the actor's head, to cover the forehead but leave the nostrils and mouth uncovered.
2. You will need to fold the front film up to keep them comfortable.
3. Do this twice, keeping it smooth. Pat it down on the top of the head and the nape.
4. Release the ears by cutting carefully into the cling film, in front of and behind the ears. Cut over a comb or doofer so the scissors do not touch the person's ears. Fold away the excess film.
5. Push the film flat to the head all round, especially above and in front of the ears and over the hairline.
6. Check that all the hair has been covered by film, add smaller bits if necessary.
7. Cover all the cling film with sticky tape or clear parcel tape.
8. Go to step 10 in 'Using a polythene bag or hairdresser's cap'.

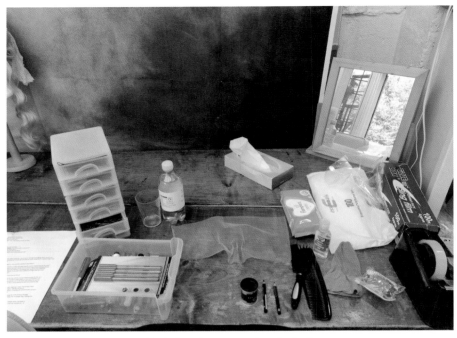

Tools for taking your client's shell.

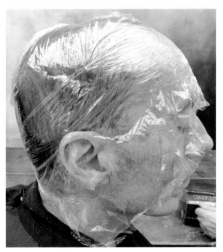

Head wrapped with cling film including eyebrows and nape.

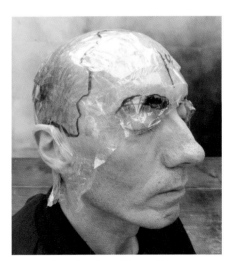

Ears freed, hairline added.

USING A POLYTHENE BAG OR HAIRDRESSER'S CAP

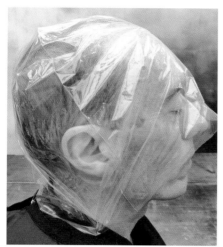

A plastic hairdressing cap in position for tape.

TOOLS:
- As for 'Cling film shell'.
- A see-through polythene bag large enough to go over the head. You can buy semi-circular disposable polythene caps/hats from hairdressing suppliers.

METHOD:
1. Cut a vertical slit in one side of the bag, where it will sit over the nose and mouth. Fold the corners of the cut away and tape them down. Place the transparent polythene bag over the head. Eyes and ears are covered by the bag.
2. Ask the actor or your assistant to hold the sides down. Take several long pieces of sticky tape and go right around the head tightly, just under the bulge at the back and on to the forehead in front at a 45-degree

PRO TIP

This is a faster way as less taping is needed.

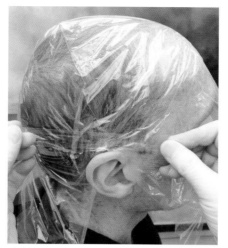

Add tape around the ears to stop the split running and create the head shape.

angle, but no need to be exact. This simply holds the bag in place while you do the rest, so your actor or helper can let go.
3. Carefully cut a slit on each side behind and in front of each ear, fold the polythene away and tape it. Add extra tape directly above and behind each ear.
4. Lay a piece of tape over the top of the head from just above each ear like headphones.
5. Lay another piece horizontally across the forehead just above the eyebrows and all the way round over the widest point of bulge.
6. Gather or fold the bag to lie flat to the nape at the back of the head. Make sure the polythene still covers all the hair, and lay on the pieces of tape horizontally one above another to hold the folds in place and make it smooth to the head.
7. Use more pieces each side of the nape to gather the bag flat between the ears and the nape, again make sure to completely cover all the hair with the edges of the bag, and lay your pieces above one another to keep it all smooth to the head.

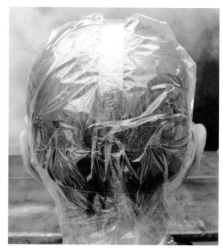

Check the nape is fully covered and seal all over with tape.

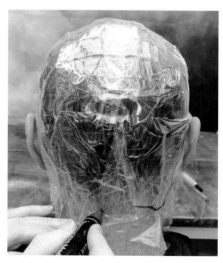

Add the actor's hairline in one colour.

8. Go back to the front and lay some more tape to flatten all the area of bag covering the forehead and down each side in front of the ears and at least 5cm behind the hairline. Cover where their hair grows, and where they recede to. Keeping this front area flat is crucial.
9. Feel free to add any extra tape so the shell will retain the shape when you lift it off the head. Add as much as you have time for, it all helps.

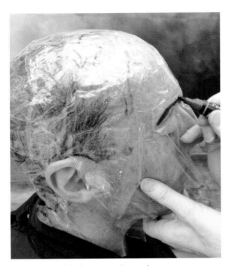

Add the actor's eyebrows.

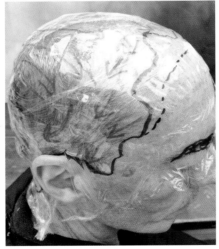

Use a different colour to add the hair directions or new hairline.

10. Take your marker pen and draw over the hairline all round. Cover this with more tape to prevent it smudging and being lost.
11. If your wig will change their hairline, mark the new required line too, but with a different colour marker pen (or dots instead of a complete line) and cover with tape.
12. Sketch in the eyebrows. Even without a fringe, this is helpful to record. If a crown, parting or break is needed, then mark that too with your pen. Add hair directions by drawing arrows.
13. Mark the centre front 'CF' and write the actor's name, including surname, over the shell. Tape over this to prevent smudging. After use, you will store them for the next time alphabetically by surname.

Removing the Shell from the Actor's Head and Making the Key

1. Stand behind them, put your hands above the ears and, if you are lucky, you can ease the shell off slowly and in one piece. If, however, it is too tight to come off, you will need to split it.

PRO TIP

If there is not much tape there, add lots more to make the section completely firm.

A straight nape key.

The best place to make the split with your scissors is vertically up the centre back, where hopefully you have already laid plenty of sticky tape. It may be better to split it over each ear; the choice depends on the shape of the shell.

KEYING THE SPLIT

In order to restore the shell after removal you will have to key the split. You will need to restore the shape to set up the wig foundation, so it is essential to get this right.

1. Use your marker pen to draw in the centre of the split section a triangle or square.

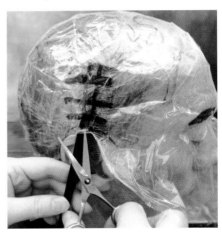

Use a comb or doofer to lift the shell away from the hair while cutting the key.

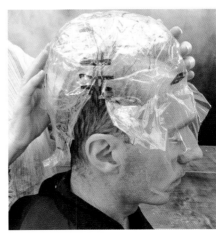

Lift off the head.

2. Now make a series of horizontal lines across the area to split.

OR

2. Draw a zigzag line so the firmly taped pieces can be interlocked again with more tape later.

3. Cut carefully upwards, over your doofer or a comb, until the shell lifts easily.

4. Remove from the client's head by lifting above the ears or from forehead to nape depending on position of slits.

5. After removal, unpin the wig cap and release any hair prep and tidy their hair, check there are no marker pen marks on their skin.

6. Thank them and check if there is anything more you should know about the wig before they leave.

Blocking Up Using a Shell with a Key

The cling film and plastic bag shells may need a key. If the shell has been keyed to open at the back, it will slip on easily.

1. If it will not slide on, you may need to key it – that is, to mark and open the back 5cm or more until it goes on.

2. When the shell is on the block, hold it with a few pins. Begin to check the fit.

3. Adjust by removing the shell and adding padding where you have noticed it is baggy.

4. Seal the padding with parcel tape until the shell sits tightly and smoothly on the block while you hold the key closed.

PREPARING TO MAKE A WIG FOUNDATION, STEP BY STEP

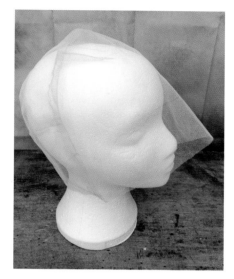

Ready-bought foundations are available in different sizes.

Making the Shell Fit the Block

1. Put your block on the wig stand upright and wrap it in a few layers of cling film to keep it clean, prevent your hook from snagging on the canvas and allow you to draw on it if you need to. When it comes to dressing your wig the cling film will keep the block dry.

PRO TIP

At this stage you may want to put a little cling film or a plastic bag over the wig stand as well to keep lacquer spray and hairs from catching in it.

Fitting the Open Foundation Shell to the Block

This step can be done in a cradle but is easier on a wig stand.

1. Check that the nape of the block is pointing away from you – there is a slightly fuller bulge at the back, or it will come to a point at the base.

2. If the block is loose on the stand, tighten your expander if there is one. If not, lay tissue or paper towel under the hole until the wig block is tight.

3. Measure the circumference of the block and check this against your notes. It would be pointless to try to fit the shell if the block measurement is much larger than your actor's head, but a small difference such as 1cm is fine and preferred by some wig makers as all foundations shrink a little in the knotting.

4. An open foundation shell will usually fit the block as there is some give in the wig lace. If there is a bulge that needs padding, lift the foundation off, add padding, re-sit the foundation until you have a fit.

5. Tape over the padding.

6. Pin the foundation to the block securely but leave the outer edges free.

7. Reach under the edges to copy the hairline on to your block with a marker pen, and add any other information, such as crown and knotting directions.

8. Take the foundation off and tape over these.

PRO TIP

Sometimes the open foundation can form the basis of the wig you are making, which is a time saver.

TO TRANSFER THE HAIRLINE TO THE BLOCK

1. Put extra parcel tape or sticky tape over the cling film on the block.
2. Put tape under the hairline, all round under the shell. Put the shell on the block to check if it is sitting on the tape, take off the shell and add more tape, as necessary. This tape will keep your block clean for future use and make marking the hairline easier if you mark it with holes.
3. When you draw the hairline, if you can, reach under the shell and draw the nape outlines over the parcel tape with a marker pen, remove the shell and lay sticky tape over the outline you have drawn. Put the shell back on the block, tape over the key lightly or pin it in place.
4. If the fit of the shell is too tight to reach under, begin making pin holes all around the hairline of the shell. Use a 1.20mm brass postiche pin and pierce the shell firmly all along the marker pen hairline at 1cm gaps. Remove the sticky tape or pins and lift off the shell.

You should be able to see your line of pin holes clearly. If not, repeat the punching or rub a little dressmaker's chalk, talc or eyeshadow into the holes. Mark the pin lines with your marker pen and seal them with tape. Check that you have added any other information, like directions for knotting, or a parting position, and taped over those.

   If you are knotting several wigs, add a small name tape to your block to remind you. Label the shell, put to one side and store for another day.

Fitting a Block Using a Keyed or Open Top Shell

1. Pad your block to meet the actor's measurements. Mark the centre lines of the block (covered in cling film, remember) with a different colour pen, by drawing along the ear-to-ear and front-to-nape measurements. Tape over the lines, which you will use to centre your work.
2. Pull the shell on as far as you can, using tape or pins to hold it securely down on the block.
3. Open any baggy area of the shell with scissors. Push in your padding, a little at a time, make it firm and as smooth as possible.
4. When you have filled the gap, tape up the opening and you are ready to start. The hairline and any other directions are already marked. Your sticky tape should stop your knotting hook penetrating the shell.

Pad your block and tape down until it meets your measurements and shell.

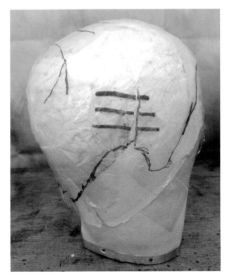

Replace shell and tape up the key.

The drag king HercuSleaze as Shakespeare. Photo and costume by HercuSleaze.

RICARDVS · III · ANG · REX ·

Making Sixteenth-Century Male Wigs and Facial Hair

4

EXAMPLE 1: FIRST TUDOR MAN – BOBBED HUMAN HAIR ON 4-PART FOUNDATION

The wig is to be full lace, hand knotted in human hair, because this is the lightest, coolest and most comfortable option.

The lace front can be stuck down for security. The hair will be hanging in a bob, so we must use real hair, which has more weight, not a fibre. A little movement in the hair will help, but no curls because of the fur collar which will matt the hair. No set-in parting, just a cross-knotted centre break on top, a bob style with a fringe.

Materials for the Wig Foundation

As with all things wig related, there are several methods, and nothing is right or wrong if it works. For this method we will use a strong, fine net for a softer and more flexible foundation. It is 61cm wide and comes in mid and dark brown, neutral, and grey. All lace is expensive; this method uses smaller pieces than some others and can be adapted to use even smaller ones.

PRO TIP

If the time or budget will not allow all-over knotting, it is possible to sew in thin weft avoiding the edges and parting.

NOTES

The costume for Richard III includes heavy layers, so the actor will be uncomfortably hot. The coat has a large fur collar, which will mess up the hair at the nape.

TOOLS:

- The block you have prepared for this actor from their shell.
- Flexible tape measure.
- Sewing scissors.
- 1m 30 denier brown foundation lace.
- 1m 20 denier flesh-coloured front lace.
- Knotting hooks.
- Dark invisible nylon thread for whipping.
- Pins: Small brass; 0.75mm nickel plated; and some with coloured heads.
- Dressmaker's chalk.
- Ribbon or tape for blocking.
- A small hammer and small pliers for those occasional times when a pin will not go in through the padding or will not come out easily.
- A doofer or piece of thin coloured card to go under the part you are knotting for visibility and to protect the shell.
- Coloured sticky notes.
- You might use weights to hold down the lace while you cut it. A sticky tape dispenser is a good shape and should be handy.

PRO TIP

- It is always better to start with too much in the way of materials and time.
- Using up smaller pieces of lace will save you money, but using larger pieces saves time.

METHOD:

1. Have your notes, pen, wig nets, tape measure, small pins, lace, thread cutting scissors, whipping hook and nylon thread handy.
2. The crossed lines on the block will now be a reference point as you try to keep your laces straight and even and the hole directions clear.

Finished lightweight four-piece foundation.

LEFT: Richard III of England with the typical bob.

MAKING THE 4-PIECE WIG FOUNDATION STEP BY STEP

Block with shell in cradle.

This is a standard, universal foundation, useful for all types of wigs. Theatre wigs are often designed to be lightweight and flexible and there's a team of people ready to repair, maintain, dismantle and re-create for the next performance. This means that their construction is not as complex as the foundations here, but these are suitable and sturdy enough to be sold or otherwise provided by freelancers.

To Make the First Nape Piece: N1

1. Take the ear to nape measurement, double it, and add on double the across-nape measurement. That is the length of the oblong strip you are going to make. It will be 5cm wide. The extra centimetres from doubling the nape measurement allow you to pleat it over the ears and fold it at the corners as you change direction. It should be long enough to sit on the block from above the ear, down to the nape on one side, across the

nape and up to above the ear the other side.
2. Add an extra 3cm to the calculated width to allow for seams.
3. Use your flexible tape measure against the shell to double check that this measurement will be long enough, before cutting out. The dominant lines in the lace should run along the shorter width of the strip.

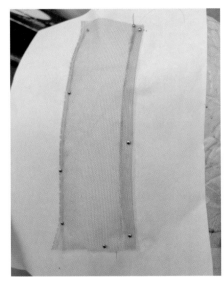

Steps 1-4: N1 cut out and 5mm seam turned over.

4. Cut this strip 8cm wide, neatly.
5. Pin one narrow end of the strip onto the block near the top.
6. Begin to fold up one long side of the lace by 1.5cm and tuck in the edge by 5mm to make a neat seam. Pin it down to the block. Do this for as far as you can down the block.

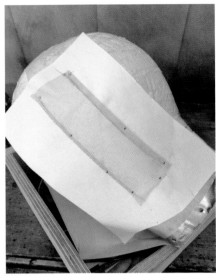

Step 5: Pin to block by narrow edge.

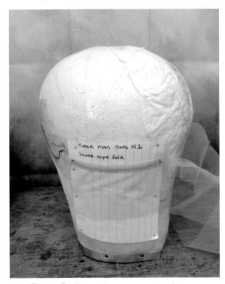

Step 6: Turn the seam, pin down.

Step 7: Whip the seam with nylon thread.

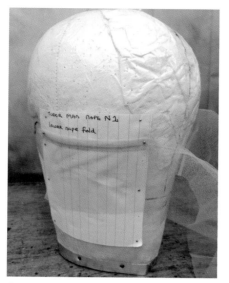

Step 8: Unpin N1, move to paper-covered area and re-pin for whipping.

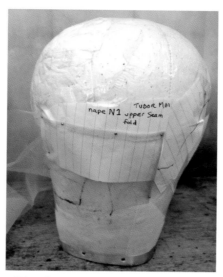

Step 9: Turned over N1 pinned to top of block.

Step 12: Mark the centre with a pin.

7. Take a matching colour of invisible nylon thread and whip this seam. (The photo shows a contrasting nylon thread to make it obvious.)

8. When there is no more paper-covered area underneath, unpin the strip, move it up the block, re-pin it over paper, fold the rest of the seam, pin that down and whip it.

9. Take the strip off the block, turn it over and pin the top to the block as before.

Steps 10 & 11: Long side with 5mm fold being whipped.

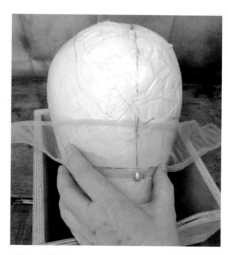

Step 13: Lay this centre marker over the centre of the nape.

10. On the other long side of the lace, make a single 5mm fold.
11. Whip that down all the way.
12. Take the strip off the block and fold it in half, with the larger seam inside, and put a pin there to mark the centre or use dressmaker's chalk.
13. Lay the strip across the nape of the shell with the centre mark over the centre front-to-nape line you drew earlier.
14. The hem should sit just below the

nape outline, as the wig will shrink a little in the knotting. The bottom edge is now smooth, with a neat hem set against the block, on the inside.
15. Pin it down every centimetre or so to the corners.
16. Make a fold as you turn up towards

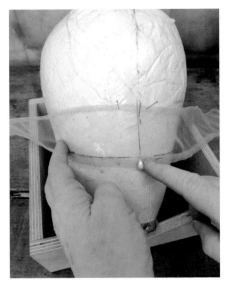

Step 14: The lower nape seam is below the nape outline.

Step 15: Pin down every centimetre to the corners.

Step 16: Make a fold as you turn up towards the ear. Pin flat to nape.

Step 17: Place and pin the folds smoothly.

Step 18: Neatly fold or curve as you change direction.

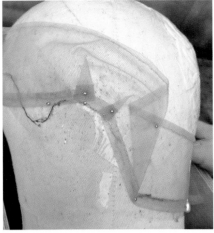

Step 19: The folds are strong enough for blocking up but smooth and flat to the head.

Step 20: Whip down with nylon thread.

Whipping close up.

each ear. Pin the fold down flat on each side of the nape.

17. Continue to place your strip and pins.

18. When the ear to nape line reaches the ears there should be enough strip

PRO TIP

Remember, the lace lines go from front
to back across the nape.

left to make a neat fold or curve as
you change direction again.

19. These folds give strength just at the
points where the wig will be pinned
to the block for dressing, but should
not be bulky. You can make several
smaller folds if it looks flatter, even
rounding the corners of the nape.

20. Whip them down with the nylon
thread.

To Make the Second Nape Piece: N2

1. For the next section (N2), we need a
piece of the same lace which will
have the dominant lines going
vertically from the front of the block
to the back.

2. Measure the distance from the top of
the piece of lace above the ear, to a
point level with the nape. The
second length you need is the
distance across the back between the
ear points. Add a 4cm seam

allowance to this measurement.

3. Cut out this piece and fold it in half.

4. Match your pin or chalk mark to the
centre line where it meets N1 on the
top seam, not the bottom edge.

5. Hang the bottom edge of the N2
lace over the N1 upper edge by
1.5cm and pin it down.

6. Keeping on the perpendicular centre
line, move up to the top edge of the
piece and pin that.

7. Work horizontally across the top
edge, out from the centre point,

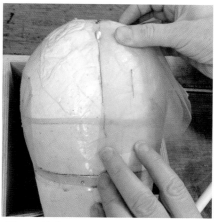

Steps 2-4: Cut out piece laid to overlap
N1 by 1.5cm.

Step 7a: Fold out from the centre until
you meet N1 over the ears.

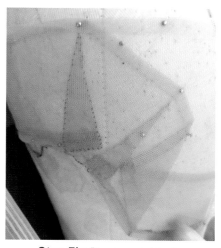

Step 7b: Pin down to block.

Step 1: Measure with holes/lines
vertically.

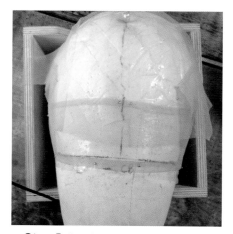

Step 5: Pin down keeping the centre
lines matched.

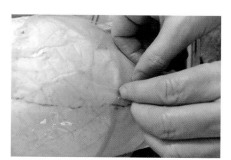

Step 8: Work out from centre, pinning
smoothly to block.

Step 9b: Pin and whip with a 'doofer' underneath for visibility.

making a 0.5cm fold towards you and pinning to the block until you meet the top edge of the first piece of lace (N1) over the ears.

8. Move back down the centre line to the bottom edge of N2, where it overlaps the top edge of N1. From the centre where you have already

Step 9c: Whipped tucks.

pinned it, work out towards each side, pinning it to lie smoothly against the block.

9. Take in the excess lace with tucks, evenly distributed each side. Pin them. Whip them.

10. Whip the tucks then trim the lace neatly at the sides to leave an even 2cm overlap all round.

11. Fold half of this under to make a 1cm seam. Pin it down as you move around the join.

12. Whip the bottom edge fold to the nape strip (N1).

13. Whip another line 1cm above, making two neat rows.

14. Go back up to the top of the lace (N2) and whip the horizontal edge down along the 0.5cm seam you pinned in a fold towards you.

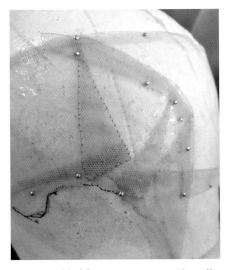

Steps 10-14: Leave a 2cm overlap all around. Fold under to make a 1cm seam. Whip it down so you have two neat rows.

To Make the Third Nape Piece: N3

1. The third piece of lace (N3) is bigger. It will sit over the crown of the head and reach close to the front hairline, so the measurement you need is the ear to ear, over the top of the head for the width, and the front to nape minus 10cm for the length. This includes the seam allowances. Cut this out neatly.

2. The front-to-nape length is the direction of the dominant lace lines. Lay from front-to-nape direction on the block, parallel with the centre line.

3. Fold the lace in half along the dominant line, mark the centre at the bottom with a pin. Match this pin with the centre line on the block, where it meets the top of the semi-circular section (N2) you have just completed.

4. Slide it down, leaving a 2cm overlap for the seam. Pin it.

5. Put in some more pins as you move back up towards the centre front to stop the lace sliding from side to side. Keep the lace lines parallel with the centre line of the block as you move up towards the front edge with pins.

6. Smooth the lace down towards the ears on each side and pin it. Move back a little, smoothing but not stretching, and pin wherever you meet the other laces.

7. Take the excess lace into several tucks or folds at each side and pin them down. Use your doofer underneath and whip them.

8. Trim the edge where this lace meets N1 and N2 so there is a 2cm overlap. Fold this under, making a 1cm seam, pin and whip it. Use a second whipping line to hold the upper edge of the underneath laces to the upper lace. All these whipped seams give the foundation strength and there will be no raw edges to fray inside the wig foundation.

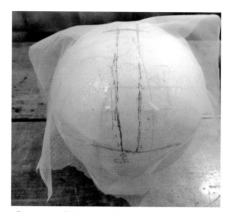

Steps 1 & 2: Cut N3 for the crown and lay from front to nape along centre lines.

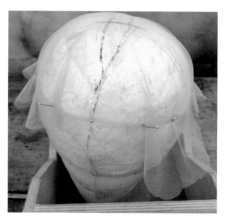

Steps 3-5: Fold the lace, marking CB at bottom. Leave a 2cm overlap and pin.

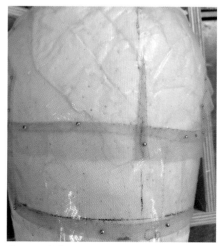

Steps 6 & 7: Smooth the lace into tucks either side, pin and whip.

Step 8: Trim lace to 2cm overlap, fold under and whip.

Left-ear profile view of tucks and seams.

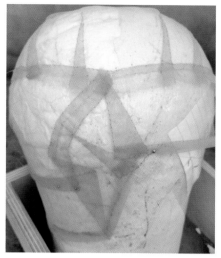

Right-ear profile view of tucks and seams.

To Make the Lace Frontal Fourth Piece: LF

The final section is the front lace; for this you can use 20 denier fine nylon lace in a flesh colour to suit the actor's skin.

1. Measure the length of hairline in front of the ears twice, plus the ear-to-ear measurement, plus 10cm for blocking. Measure along the dominant line of the lace and sit it at right angles to the top of the wig. You will need at least 7cm in front of the hairline to sit over the forehead and 10cm behind. Cut your front lace piece.

2. Hold and centre the lace as before, but mark with chalk. Place the centre point of front lace, with lines going from side to side, smoothly on the centre front line where it crosses the hairline.

3. Hold it with one hand while you put two pins behind, where it overlaps the top of the third section of foundation lace and another two pins in the front, near the edge of the lace furthest over the forehead, to hold it.

4. Keep holding your hand over the

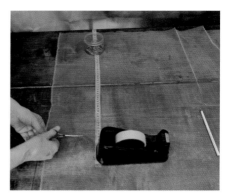

Step 1: Cutting the lace with weights.

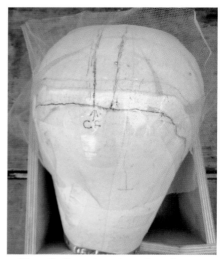

Step 2: Smooth and pin front lace in place.

Step 4: Tuck the top so it lies smooth to the crown and ears.

centre front, rather than putting more pins in to the lace, ease each side of the lace outwards along the dominant lines, to join the rest of the foundation above the ears. Pin it on each side. The lace in the area in front of the ears should be stroked back smoothly and several pins put in to hold it.

5. The top is more difficult. You will need to make tucks to control the spare lace, but do not let them reach the hairline. As there is a break, keep that clear of tucks too. Where two laces meet there will be a seam, but you can either do a simple overlap and whip two lines or tuck the edge of the top lace under to make a neat finish. The important thing is not to have any bulky seam here where it is most likely to be seen.

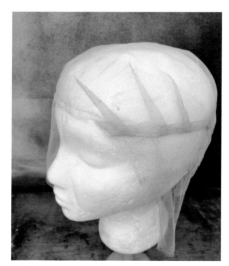

Step 5: Tuck the top so it avoids the hairline and break. Whip.

PRO TIP

Remove the front pins that are holding the front lace down. This will make the cotton line easier to insert.

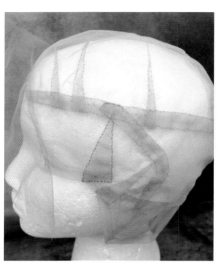

Steps 6 & 7: Take off block, turn inside out, whip seams.

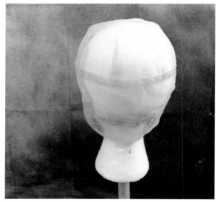

Step 8: Check the fitting.

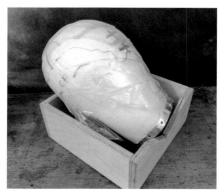

Blocked up and ready to knot!

6. Use your shell or outline in contrasting colour to the hair you will be using and run in a cotton line over the marker pen lines on the block to mark the hairline, crown, parting or any other helpful directions, and tie it off securely. Carefully remove all the remaining pins and take the new foundation off the block.

7. Check that all your seams and folds are well whipped, as it is possible to miss parts. You need to turn the foundation inside out to check. Block it up inside out to whip any areas of seam or tuck that you have missed.

8. Put the foundation back on the block the right way round and check that it still fits.

KNOTTING THE WIG

Blocking Up

1. Fold the foundation in half, front to nape and mark the centre on the lace with chalk.

2. Put a large pin in this mark on the top of the foundation and centre it

on the block, moving the pin till you have it in position.

3. Use a large pin over each ear and at the sides of the nape to hold the foundation.

4. Check that the cotton line and nape seam are on the hairline. Take out the original pin on top.

5. Use the smallest pins over a tape to hold the fine front lace down. Use other small pins all around the edges of the wig to hold it firmly to the block. This is important for making tight knots. You cannot knot well on baggy lace.

LENGTH OF HAIR

1. Measure from the centre top of the wig to the bottom of the foundation at the nape. It may for instance be 35cm.

2. Allow 5cm for knotting, so choose hair that is at least 40cm long, of the right colours.

3. Prepare the mats with the roots towards your right. It is a good idea to write 'Roots' on to both your wire

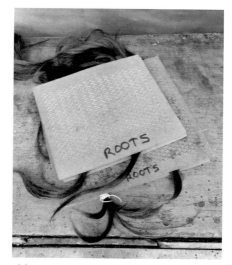

Mats with mixed hair, roots-end labelled as such.

Human hair in wefts or tied with thread at the root end. Use different colours and lengths for a natural appearance and to save resources.

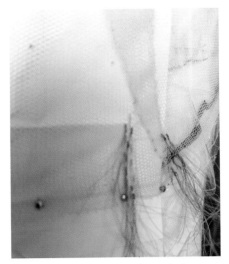

Close-up of nape and side triple-knots.

mats when they arrive, at the end where the wires are bent away from you.

4. The hair may come as a bundle of weft or a bundle of loose hair tied with soft string, usually tapestry wool. Keep some for tying up loose hair.

5. To release the hair from weft, cut it as close to the woven strings as you can. Hold it tightly 6cm from the cut end and comb out the short ends. Lay the hair into the mats, cut end/roots towards the right. Only release 20cm at a time from the weft, so the mats are not overloaded.

6. The bundle of loose hair should be held by the roots – that is the end closest to the soft string. Hold it and cut into the top of the string, just enough to unwind it from around the hank. Halve the bundle, lay down the half to begin work with, remembering which is the root end.

7. Use the string to re-tie the spare half bundle and move it away for later.

8. Lay down the hair you are about to use on the lower wire mat, roots to the right, wires bent away to the left. Smooth out any kinks. Spread the hair so it is not a thick pile. Put the

other mat on top; do this from directly on top, so as not disturb the hair. Use a small weight like a sticky tape dispenser to hold the mats down. Do not use anything heavier or the hair will stretch as you pull it through.

9. Never reverse the front hairs, as a reversed knot looks bigger. However, from about five holes in, you can usually reverse knot and this will give some bounce to the dressing. It also means that when you are knotting the back and meet up with the front, the hair will be lying away from you.

10. For this wig, you will knot the front lace sides first. The hair will hang down, if the lace holes allow, or slightly back towards the ears. There

will be no reverse knotting on the sides of the front lace. The first five holes nearest the cotton line will be single hairs; the rest can be two hairs.

11. Start at the bottom edge of the hairline in front of the ears. Two holes in front of the cotton line, knot one hair at a time, every three holes. Just inside the cotton line, do the same, staggering the holes to be one hole away from the ones in front.

12. Knot the whole of that front lace section, working upwards for about 8cm on each side. Use two hairs per knot and keep each knot two holes away from the nearest other knot.

13. This wig has no parting. The hair will hang from a centre break. This is marked by a cotton line or the marker pen line if you are working directly on the shell. The fringe will break from 5cm back from the centre front.

14. Re-position the block so you can work on the centre front. Knot towards each side, one hair at a time, two holes in front of the cotton line, and knot every three holes. These knots will be angled by the

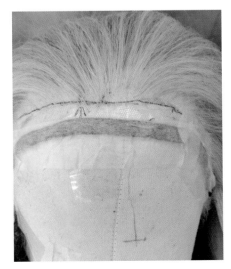

Knotting hair directions.

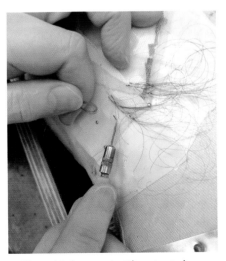

Keep this loop wet with water to keep knots tight.

lines in the lace to lie out, for the fringe, onto what will be the actor's face, like the rays of the sun. At the sides, the front hair will lay over the earlier knotting.

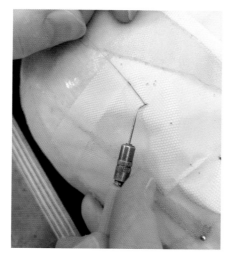

Tight double knot.

PRO TIP

Take your time around visible areas. Dip the loop of the hair between thumb and forefinger in water to keep your knots fine and tight.

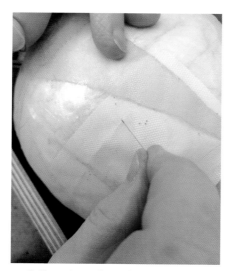

Pulling through two-hairs at a time.

15. In the centre front of the fringe, the knots will lie in alternate directions in a 5cm area, some to the left and some to the right. As before, keep two holes away from other knots and knot single hairs just behind the cotton line. Increase to two hairs in each knot and fill the front lace of the wig. Comb the hair as you go along.

    This is delicate lace, so be careful not to tear it.

    If you make a fat knot by accident, use your hook to open it and discard the hair.

    If you make an incomplete knot, where only part of the hair has come through, take one loose end and pull gently – the hair will slide out.

    Hair from incomplete knots will stick up in the air and soon fall out, better to lose them now than have thin patches.

16. At the end of your marked break line, on the crown of the head, choose one side of N3 and begin to knot. These are two-hair knots, with some single hair. They are reversed and you will cross the directions for 2cm wide over the break line. This

Holding back hair and tightening a knot.

These shorter hairs are the roots.

PRO TIP

When you are more confident, you can use shorter hair for the nape; this saves time and money.

combination will help give a natural bounce to the hair. Like the front, once completed, the directions will flow out to hang forward and join the front and sides.

17. When you have completed this crossed and reversed section, the hard work is over, and the wig half completed. Pat yourself on the back. Pin the top hair into a pin curl or elastic to keep out of your way.

18. At this point re-arrange your block to knot the nape. As we know there will be a large fur collar in the costume; this nape hair is going to get sweaty. The moisture will cause the hair to swell and loosen the knots. To alleviate this, you must double knot the nape.

19. You will not be under-knotting the wig. You do not need to knot every hole. Use two hairs in each knot and leave three holes empty all round each knot. You will find the natural

line of knotting the lace is slightly
outward towards the corners of the
nape.

Cutting Out the Roots

When the first section of the nape (N1)
has been knotted, it will need to have the
roots cut out.

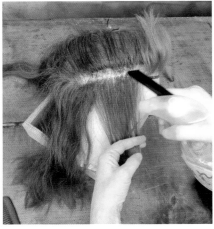

2. Damp with a spray of water.

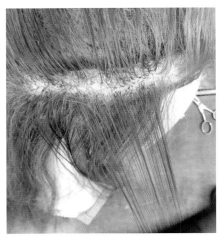

5. Comb through.

1. Comb through the section.

1. Comb the hair and use section clips
    to hold most of it out of your way.
2. Take a small section and damp it.
3. Hold the section at right angles to
    the wig and backcomb the hair
    firmly down to the knots.
4. Hold the longer hair in one hand
    and tease out the shorter tangled
    hair, which is the root section, and
    cut it off.
5. Comb through that piece and take
    the next and repeat.
6. The next section to knot is N2, the

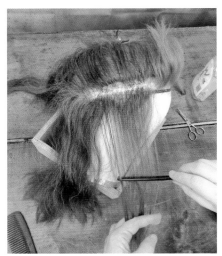

3. Backcomb.

Sewn in weft close to hairline showing if
parted incorrectly.

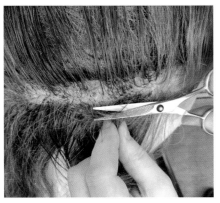

4. Cut out the roots.

Richard III before cutting.

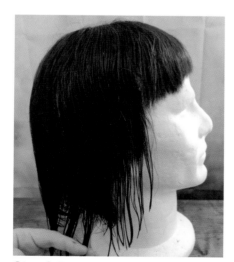

Step 4: Trim nape blunt 4cm below nape.

semi-circular section and the knots will follow the straight up and down line of the lace.

7. Finally, the top lace (N3) will be knotted to flow down into the nape hair. The 5cm wide section of hair above the ears will need to be more densely knotted than the rest of the wig to cover them. Check the whole wig for colour and thickness, take it off the block and check inside, again for thickness.

To Cut and Style the Bob Wig

BLOCK UP THE WIG

1. Be sure it is level on the block and stand.
2. Comb it through and spray lightly with water.
3. Comb through again and leave to dry naturally. This is to allow all the cuticle edges of the hair that have been roughened by the knotting hook to close and recover.

PREPARING AND CUTTING THE HAIR

1. Section fist-sized areas of the wig into clumps with section clips, leaving 5cm deep at the nape exposed.
2. Damp this, halve it horizontally and clip up the top section.
3. Make three vertical sections and clip them; that is, a section each side of the nape and one in the middle. The middle section will be your base line.
4. The base line will be 4cm below the nape seam. Comb it down and cut it straight across.
5. Measure the distance from the cut edge of hair down to the rim of the wig block and mark this all round the sides with colour-headed pins pushed into the block.
6. Now put in another row of pins, 4cm below that, at the sides and front. These lines are to save you from

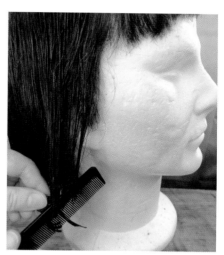

Step 6: Trim graduating upwards in a slope.

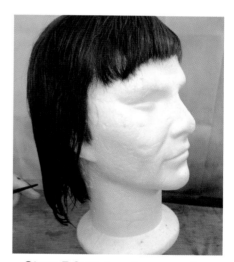

Steps 7-9: Club cutting repeated on both sides.

cutting the sides unevenly. The lower second row is the allowance for protruding ears. Where the lines part, join the lower pin line gradually to the upper with a little slope, so there is not a sudden break in the hair lengths.

7. Release a side of nape section, comb it down to the lower pin line and cut straight across, following the slope. Club cutting a wig is easier than on a person as there is less hair, but you

Step 10: Trim the fringe.

may still have to take smaller sections to get a clean cut.

8. Repeat on the other side of the nape.
9. Work your way up the wig in small, horizontal sections, pulling the damp hair down to the pin line and cutting. Leave the fringe till last.
10. There should be an eyebrow line marked on your shell to guide you with fringe cutting. Put in colour-headed pins on each brow as

marked, then more pins to join them and across to the hairline.

11. Comb the fringe hair, damp it and make three sections. Pin up the sides.
12. Take the centre section and halve it horizontally.
13. Pin up the top half.
14. Comb and cut the bottom half, pulling it down below the pin line as it will rise as it dries.
15. Repeat with the lower half of the other two fringe sections.
16. Cut the upper sections in the same way.

STYLING THE WIG

1. As you comb through the damp wig, pull slightly on the ends of the hair to guide them under and let them dry naturally in that rounded-under shape.
2. For a more finished look, use curling tongs to turn the ends of hair under more directly. The root lengths will not need touching.

Finished First Tudor Man, Richard III.

EXAMPLE 2: SECOND TUDOR MAN

This sort of wig could be a complete disguise if an actor is playing several parts in the play. This style of short wig

Step 1: Comb and turn the hair and allow to dry naturally.

Turned under with fingers.

Second Tudor Man reference: *Portrait of a Young Scholar*, 1597, Rubens.

is a versatile and useful addition that will work as well in Roman plays such as *Julius Caesar* and *Anthony and Cleopatra* as in the history plays, and it can be paired with any style of facial hair.

Making Facial Hair 1: Beard and Moustaches

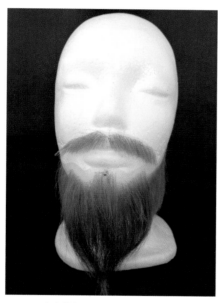

A full beard and moustache.

MEASURING FOR FACIAL HAIR
See Appendix I: Facial Hair Measurement Form.

- If you are working remotely, you can use the measurement form in the Appendix and simply ask the actor to measure themselves.
- Take the measurements in millimetres and it is difficult to go wrong.
- Taking a shell of the lower half of their face ensures that you have all the dimensions in an easy-to-understand piece and it will be far easier to perfect.

TAKING A BEARD SHELL
The aim with all methods is to make a solid shell that will not flop out of shape when taken off the face.

TOOLS:
- Sticky tape in a dispenser.
- Scissors.
- Three colours of marker pen.
- Hair colour swatches.
- Tape measure.
- Note pad and pen or digital version.
- Camera (probably on phone but beware of data protection).
- Spray bottle filled with water and a little conditioner.
- Beard laces.
- Eyebrow pencils and sharpener.
- Small pins.
- Cling film in a dispenser, or a thin polythene sheet, or even part of a bag.

OR
- Pre-prepared beard lace in a suitable but oversized shape.

A PLASTIC SHELL
1. Wear a face mask for working this close. Pull your own hair back off your face with a clip or elastic. Put the actor's own hair behind their ears, or clip or pin it back from the face too.
2. Seat your actor on a raised chair so you do not have to strain your back while taking the shape. Explain to the actor what you are about to do and how you will go about it. Ask if there is anything about the beard

and moustache that you should know, and whether you can take their photograph for reference.
3. They may only need a section of facial but take the full shell as a record in case there is a change of plan.
4. Check your hair colour swatches for reference with the actor's own colour.
5. Having their mouth covered can be stressful, so agree that a raised hand or similar signal will let you know they are in distress and you need to remove the cling film. They may just need to cough! They may prefer to hold it themselves, which works well for you too!

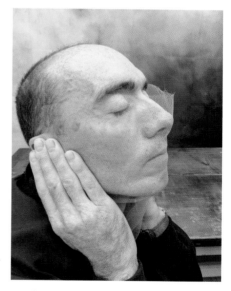

Actor holding the lace themselves.

CLING FILM
As this pesky stuff can be stickier than you expect, it is useful to have a second pair of hands to take a section from the roll and hand it to you. Sticky tape will

PRO TIP

The actor could hold the shell on the face. Let them know if you need this help before you begin.

be easier to handle if someone else cuts sections to give you. Parcel tape is a little too inflexible for this.

1. Take a large section of cling film at least 65cm wide, because you will want to wrap it all the way round the head under the eyes so it sticks to itself at the back.
2. Make slits in the film when you can approximate where the nose and mouth are. Do this well away from your actor, with small scissors pointed into fresh air between you and the actor's face. Although you are taking care not to cover the nostrils, remember you need a pattern from the moustache area as well so ensure this area and below the mouth are smooth.
3. Join the cling film to itself at the back.
4. Repeat to get a stronger shell at least one, if not three times more.
5. Press it smooth to the face and gather

the excess under the chin. It should sit slightly behind the base of the ears and sit well down on the neck. You may need an extra piece of film for the neck, or to cover the actor's own sideburns.

METHOD 1: QUICK SHELL
The flat side of a clear polythene bag may be easier to deal with than cling film and requires less sticky tape, so is a faster method. Make a centre split for the nose, then lay it on as you would the smaller piece of cling film and ask the actor to hold the sides tightly, flat to their face, while you tape under the jaw for a snug fit. Then draw on the shape as below, taking it in turns with the actor to hold each side while you work.
OR
If you have help, place a large piece of cling film, 37cm wide, across the face below the nostrils but covering the mouth and reaching all the way from ear to ear. It should go slightly behind the base of the ears and sit well down on the neck and cover their own sideburns. You may need an extra piece of film for this. Press it smooth to the face and gather the excess under the chin.

Take small pieces of sticky tape (big ones wrap round themselves) and cover all the cling film, especially underneath where there are several layers in the tucks.

METHOD 2: BEARD LACE
Less stressful for the actor is to fit a ready-made beard lace.

1. Make several of different sizes and colours in advance. It need only have two tucks in the chin to indicate how to position it.

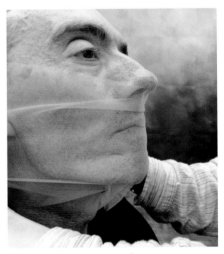
Lace beard shell with tucks under chin.

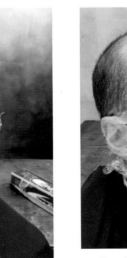
Cling film beard shell.

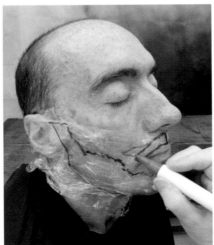
Beard shell with tape and shape of hairline in blue and styling in red.

Drawing the shape with an eyebrow pencil.

2. Ask the actor or your assistant to hold it there while you make any adjustments with a few pins.
3. Mark the hairline with an eyebrow pencil and the position of the mouth with a different colour pencil.

Drawing the Shape

1. Use one colour of marker pen to indicate the outline of the lips, the position of the nostrils and the actor's own sideburn area up to the top of the ear. You might want to add the line of the nasolabial fold from mouth to nose and the puppet line from mouth to jaw, as these are the areas of greatest movement.
2. Even if a full beard is not required, use another colour of marker pen to draw their own natural growth, using a dotted line all round. This is still a useful reference.
3. With a third colour of marker pen, draw on the required shape of beard and moustache to be made with a solid line.
4. Go right up to their own sideburns and all the way round under the chin.
5. Cover all marker pen with sticky tape. Write the actor's name on the shell and tape over it.
6. Estimate where the finished beard should hang to and measure from the bottom lip to find this length. Make a note under the beard measurements form.

Blocking Up the Shell

TOOLS:
- Shell.
- Beard/Chin Block – preferably cork-filled canvas covered and made for the purpose.
- Padding.
- Sticky tape.

Adapted polystyrene chin block.

- Pins.
- Scissors.
- Polystyrene head for display and photography.

Polystyrene heads could be adapted to knot on in a pinch.

The 'female' polystyrene heads generally have too small a jaw and they have necks that angle out from under the chin to a wide base, interfering with knotting. Cut that off.

The 'male' block often has a slightly wider lip at the base, which helps it to stand upright, but will catch on your hook as you work, so be prepared to cut this off. The 'man' shape has a larger, square jaw, but you will almost certainly still need to pad it to fill your shell.

METHOD:
1. Cover the block with cling film and sticky tape to avoid polystyrene balls shedding.
2. Working on a polystyrene head can be frustrating as they are not heavy enough to counteract the tension when you make a knot, they just lift

from the stand or cradle. The head will need tying down to your knotting cradle above and below the chin. It helps to cut grooves for your string to prevent it from slipping off. Alternatively, a weight can be stuck to the rear of the block.

A workable chin can also be built up on a silicone hairdressing training head or a regular canvas wig block using padding and tape, but neither this nor the polystyrene head will be as easy to pin into and work on as an actual cork and canvas beard block.

If you have a cork and canvas beard block, cover it in cling film and lightly pin down the shell. Pad it out for a snug fit. Tape over any padding. At this point it can be helpful to cover the chin in paper that contrasts with the wig lace and marker pen before you pin and tape down the shell itself on top for making the lace shape.

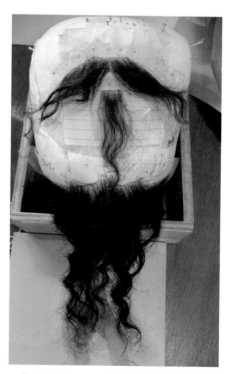

Finished moustache, thumb piece/tuft and beard.

Selecting the colour of lace.

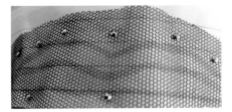

Pattern over lined paper, lace pinned down.

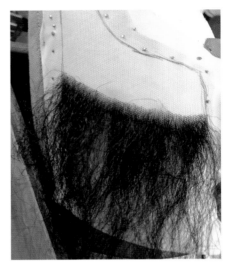

Start at the lowest part of the beard and work up.

The Moustache

The moustache can be made on an ordinary wig block, lying on its side. When making a facial set it is better to knot the moustache first, then, as your beard nears completion, you can lay the moustache in position to check colours and density match.

1. Take the pattern for the moustache from the chin block before you start to make the beard lace. This is because the moustache will be made on front lace whose lines go from side to side, in order to supply more natural growth directions for the knotting.
2. Make two copies of the pattern. This is so that you can make two moustaches close to each other to check for colour and thickness.
3. Leave the shell fixed on the block rather than trying to transfer the outline.
4. There will be two outlines; one shows the area of growth of hair and another the final outline of the dressed moustache. Do these in different colours or one solid, one dotted. You will knot inside the area

PRO TIP

- Mane-sta in California supply non-fraying front lace which makes an excellent base for moustaches. The moustaches are much longer lasting than those made on ordinary lace. Eseewig in Europe make a similar item, suitable for stage but not film, or use Fray Stop on the lace before you knot it.

- Always offer to make two moustaches for a beard, in case one is lost or damaged. Understudies will expect to wear their principal's wig, if it fits and is appropriate, but facial is always specific to each actor, for sanitary reasons.

of growth of hair.
5. Select the correct colour of lace.
6. Cover the pattern on the block, ensuring it is even and the holes travel in the right directions.
7. Do not reverse the knotting. Use single hairs as the larger knots will be more evident on a moustache. The lower jawline of a beard can take two hairs.
8. Start knotting from the lower outside edge on each side and work inwards and upwards, checking as you go that the sides match.

Use this technique on eyebrows as well.

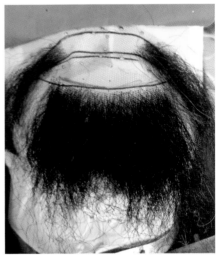

Keep comparing sides to ensure the correct colour and gradient.

PRO TIP

For a full, natural growth, the top edge is like a wig front edge, single knots with two empty holes between them on the hairline, staggered in the top two rows. Below that is fine knotting with hairs in alternate holes for two rows and below that a hair in every hole and every row.

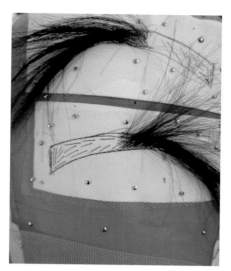

Eyebrows can be made in the same way.

Beard Tuft

This sits immediately below the bottom lip and will be a separate item. The lace lines go up and down like the beard and the knots are single hairs, every hole, no 'front edge' thinning.

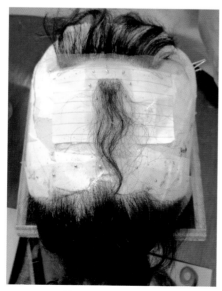

Separate beard tuft.

Making the Beard

For a leading actor, this full beard is sometimes made in three sections, chin and two side pieces, for extra flexibility. This takes slightly longer to glue on than a one piece and is not suitable for quick changes. Knot it in three sections as chin beard and sideburns, using your pattern.

TOOLS:
- Half a metre front lace, to suit actor's skin colour.
- Hair or fibre as appropriate in colour and as short as possible.
- Dressmaker's chalk.
- Pins.
- Whipping nylon to match lace.
- Knotting hook.
- Cradle.
- Scissors.
- A little saucer of water.

METHOD:
1. Add a vertical centre line to the shell with a marker pen and tape over it before making the lace shape.
2. Measure the beard to see how much lace you will need. It is usually a rectangle, approx. 36cm across between the ears and about 25cm from the top of the sideburns to the Adam's apple. The 25cm measurement is taken along the dominant lines in the lace, as they will go straight up and down on the beard and the actor's face.
3. Fold the lace in half, mark the centre and lay the lace on your chin block, lines vertical, sitting on the centre mark of the shell, sides sitting above the top of the sideburn line.
4. Pin in above the top line of the outline, in the centre, and at either side of the mouth and beneath the chin. These are to stop the lace drifting to one side and making the beard crooked.
5. Smooth the lace towards each ear at

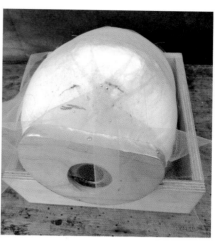

Tucks under the chin.

Knot stopper spray is applied before styling.

the sides and pin it down all round.
6. Tip the chin block up so you can see under the chin. Gather the excess lace under the centre of the chin and distribute it evenly into small, flat tucks. Pin and whip these down.

Hair for Facial Pieces

Some fibres will break if dressed with beard irons, so if the item is for someone else to maintain, be sure you have made

PRO TIP
Fibre can be used in facial but check that it will not dissolve in acetone as the facial will be cleaned each time it is worn.

it clear in the record what materials you have used.

Very coarse hair like tail yak will not tie tight knots on fine lace and is better woven and sewn in if needed for a special effect or extra length. Use something softer for the rest of the beard.

Mix your beard hair with as much care as the wig. If the facial needs to look rough it is often a case of styling and product rather than using coarse hair. The beard may be designed to be a different colour from the wig as this is still a natural look, but there should be some colour connection.

The sideburns' top edges should match the wig for colour and density, then thin out as they cross towards the mouth. Cheaper hair can generally be used for shorter beards like this but is often bulked out with odd wire-like hairs, which must be discarded as they will not make a knot and some fine, brittle hairs which break when you try to knot them. Pre-curled hair, cheaply bought as weft, is ideal for this.

PRO TIP

When trimming wigs, always hold on to any hair long enough to knot even if the roots and points are mixed, as you may be able to use it up on short facial pieces.

Knotting the Beard

1. Lay out your hair in the mats. At least three colours should be used, something darker streaked or mixed in below the chin, something lighter mixed into the top hairline, and the basic colour which itself is usually a mix, near the wig.
2. Although some natural beards appear uniformly dense, ours will look more natural if we also vary the density. Thinning the beard hair by

A 'Jack Sparrow' set with separate beard tuft.

spacing out the knots where it grows up the cheeks on each side helps and there is often a thinning or bald area just below the beard tuft, above the chin.

Step 1: Dampened beard.

3. Start knotting with the awkward area, possibly with tucks, under the chin. The hairs will lie down towards the neck so start at the lowest edge and work up towards the chin point. As they will not be seen and this is usually some of the thickest hair growth, use two hairs and knot almost every hole.
4. Once that is out of the way you can start to work your way around the jaw line, and upwards onto the cheeks. Knots will be alternate holes and all single hairs.
5. Pull knots tight and double check for unwanted density changes, colour differences or big knots. Sort them all out before going further.
6. Use a knot stopper spray afterwards. Let it dry.

Styling the Beard and Moustache

PRE-STYLING

Keep the moustache and beard tuft separate for now and dress the beard first.

1. Damp the hair and comb through with some light styling crème or conditioner. If you have used pre-permed hair, little more needs to be done beside a final trim after you have styled the moustache and tuft. Otherwise, do not start your first haircut until you have put in some curl.

CURLING THE HAIR

All the usual techniques are available to you; curling tongs, rollers, pin curls, perming curlers and so on. (*See* the section on curling synthetic hair in Chapter 5, Example 2: Tudor Woman). Wahl and several other manufacturers produce a mini electric tong with thermostat, dual heat and a swivelling cord and most importantly a diameter of 1cm, ideal for facial hair and essential kit.

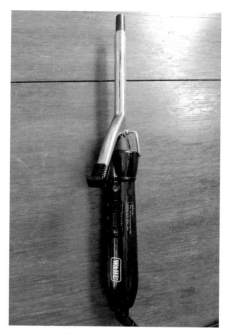

Electric beard tongs.

Beard oven – avoid!

Styling twirled ends with pins and gel.

Styled moustache.

2. Damp and curl the beard hair in the direction of the natural beard growth by taking small sections and setting them on small red bendies with wire insides, perm rollers and pins, or your finger.
3. Dry in the wig oven.
4. While they are drying, roller the beard tuft and moustache as you did the beard.
5. When they all dried (and cooled if they came out of the oven) take the rollers out of the beard and comb it all through in the direction in which it will lie.

6. Start from the centre of the chin and check the measurement of the curled hair with that required, trimming off any excess.
7. It is best to do this by holding the hair up, away from the block at a right angle as you cut. When you release the hair the layers will each be slightly above the ones below and avoid the strange look of a blunt-cut beard.
8. Trim the moustache and tuft to fit the patterns you have taken.
9. Some moustaches need extra work at this point, depending on the style. The fashion for facial in Elizabethan times was for something smaller, the moustache ends pointed with a wax that could be coloured and scented. This is better replicated with a little PVA glue or spirit gum, which will not smudge on to the face if there is close contact.
10. Pin the tuft and moustache onto the beard block to check the length and style in their real position and adjust if needed.
11. Trim the lace.

EXAMPLE 2: SECOND TUDOR MAN'S SHORT WIG

Richard Drake, 1535–1603, similar to our Second Tudor Man's short wig with moustache, beard tuft and beard.

Method to Make a Three-Piece Wig Foundation for a Short-Haired Wig

Skulls come in many shapes and sizes. This is a suitable foundation-making method for a skull that is relatively square, without a pronounced bulge at the back over the occipital bone and with a wide neck. This is slightly faster to make than the four-piece type. However, the triple knotted nape takes a little more time to do, so things even out.

This wig will be the shortest hair length (usually 8in or 20cm is the

shortest available from suppliers), knotted forward from a crown and the nape hair itself will be triple knotted to lay flat.

MAKING THE FOUNDATION

1. Set up your shell on the block with centre line, crown and knotting directions marked, and your hair in the mats, with your tools (*see* Making the Four-Piece Foundation), including flexible tape measure and dressmaker's chalk.
2. The first piece of foundation lace, Width 1 (W1), is an oblong, matched

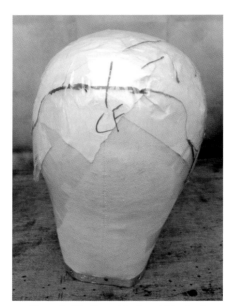

Step 1: Shell, padded and blocked.

Steps 2-3: Measure and cut the lace with selvedge.

either to the actor's flesh tone or the hair colour. Measure half the front-to-nape distance along the dominant lines of the lace. This will sit on the centre line of the shell. The width will be the temple to temple measurement and should be a selvedge. Cut this out.
3. Pin it to a block, lines going from side to side. Fold over once by 0.5cm

and whip one long side of lace to be the upper seam.
4. Take the lace off the block. Fold the lace in half along the dominant line and mark with chalk.
5. Place this piece of lace (W1) on the shell on the block, dominant lines parallel with the centre line, front to nape and the chalk mark upon it. Seam folded towards you on the upper edge. The selvedge will be underneath, against the block and sitting just below the outline on the shell. Pin W1 onto the centre line while you work.
6. On the lower edge, at the selvedge, pin the centre over the centre line of the block.
7. From the centre of the nape, work out towards each side, making tucks in the lace as required to keep it flat to the head when you turn the corners of the nape or over the ears. Keep the tucks symmetrical, as they will influence your knotting directions. Pin and whip down all the tucks.
8. Now the second lace (W2). Cut this

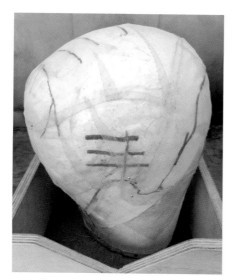

Steps 4-7: Symmetrical tucks.

piece to fit the top of the wig taking the ear to ear measurement to give us the width and half the front to nape measurement gives us the length, which is along the dominant lace lines. Fold the lace in half along the dominant lines and mark it. Lay the lace on the centre line of the shell with the lines going vertically from

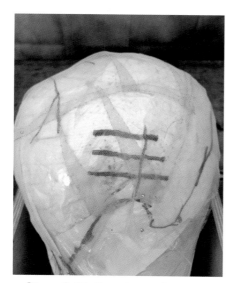

Steps 8-10: Smooth over the crown.

front to nape. The front of the lace will sit behind the hairline. The bottom will overlap the top edge of W1 by 1cm. Pin the lace along the centre line while you work on it.

9. Smooth the front edge of the lace and pin it down.
10. Go to the crown and smooth the lace down to each side from there. Go to the left and right sides of the bottom line and pin the lace to W1 on the fold. This should leave most of the top and crown smooth for knotting.
11. Work your way around making symmetrical tucks to evenly control the excess lace, pinning and whipping them over a doofer.
12. Trim the lace to leave only a 1cm overlap with W1. Turn half of that under and pin it all around. Whip this seam in two rows.
13. Go to the front of the wig and check there is a neat symmetrical line 2cm behind the hairline all round. Trim off any excess and fold 0.5cm up as a seam and whip it.
14. Lay your front lace (FL) over the hairline and centre it, pin above where it overlaps W2 and 5cm in front of the hairline. Lay one hand on

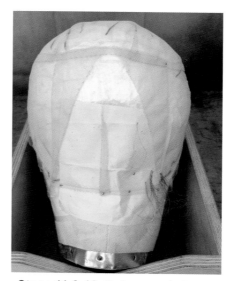

Steps 11 & 12: Tuck, pin and whip all seams.

Step 13: Check the front is neat and symmetrical.

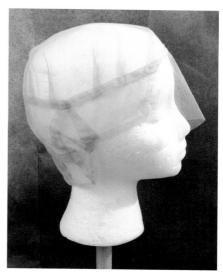

Step 16: Whipped front seam.

the centre to prevent it from moving as you smooth the lace back towards the ears following the dominant lace lines, so it lies flat in front of the ears and at the temples. Pin it.
15. Move up to the centre front and start to ease any fullness into small tucks. Pin these and whip over a doofer.
16. Check that there is only a 1cm

overlap with W2 and W1, then trim
any excess. Fold the edge under and
whip the seam.

17. Remove the pins and run in the
cotton line to mark the hairline and
the knotting directions.

18. Unblock the wig, turn it inside out
and check that all your seams are
whipped, and that the foundation
will fit back on the block without any
difficulty caused by pulling the lace
too tightly when setting up.

19. Add tabs if needed. Pin the nape on
the block inside out and add a small
piece of front lace to each side of the
nape, 2cm square. Pin and whip it.

Knotting the Short Wig

There are two special considerations
with this wig:

A. The triple knot (sometimes called the
woven knot) will keep the nape hair
lying flat. It is especially useful for a
shaven nape, or in this instance a
short nape.

B. The knotting directions on the crown
of the head. An area the size of the
palm of your hand will, if you have
marked your directions clearly, be
knotted in a swirl of reversed cross
knotting. The usual 'starfish' pattern
will look unreal on short hair and a
more natural swirl, blending into a
side break, is required.

METHOD:

1. Re-block the wig securely with
galloon on front lace. Lay micropore
over the pins in the galloon and
ensure it is holding the lace tabs at

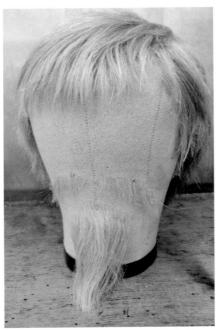

Short wig, beard and moustache.

the nape and those on the front
edge.

2. Set up your hair in mats and your
hook, comb, scissors and water spray.
Use a wig stand or cradle to support

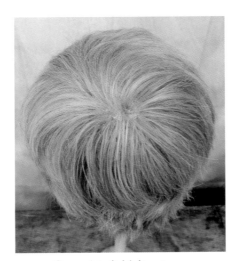

Crown 'starfish' directions.

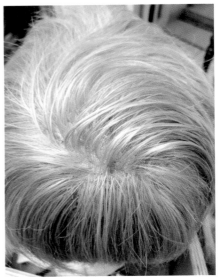

Crown swirl into break directions.

Shell with knotting directions ready.

your block. Wear an apron. The top
of this wig will be single knotted with
two hairs in alternate holes, except
on the seams where it will be double
knotted. Do not reverse any double
knotting. The nape will have the
triple knots. The front hairline and
the nape tabs will be single hairs,
single knotting.

3. Begin with the hairline, which will be single hairs knotted to lie on to the forehead from a side break. Knot staggered single hairs, two rows in front of the cotton line and two behind it. They will all be two rows and two holes apart.

4. Behind the hairline, fill in with single hairs every hole on the centre front lace, cross knotting at the break.

5. The lower side hairs will all lie downwards, but at the temple points it will angle back towards the ears slightly. Where these sides meet the forward knotted top section there will be some cross knotting.

6. On the top of the head, at the centre point of the crown, following the marked directions, reverse knot into the crown and cross knot over the break. Do this on the flat top of the head only.

7. As you work down the sides and back, do not reverse knot but there will be some cross knotting when you change direction at the sides of the front, above the ears.

8. Level with the ears, stop knotting.

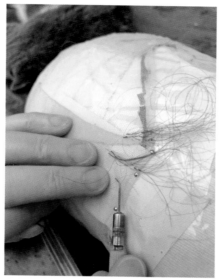

Under one lace bar.

Comb through all the knotting. Clip this hair up and out of your way while you knot the nape.

9. First single knot the tabs, every other hole, up to 1cm from nape.

10. Knot an area 2cm wide all around the nape with two hairs each in double knots, two holes apart. Comb through, damp with water spray and cut out the roots from the double knots.

11. The next section is the triple knots. Before starting this, put extra pins in your foundation 4cm above the nape knotting you have done. This is to keep the nape lace (W1) braced.

12. Take your hook, go under one lace bar as usual, then over the next bar and under a second lace bar.

13. Now pick up two hairs and make a double knot as usual and as you lay the hair down, you will see that it lies flat to the lace. Do not gather up the lace by pulling too hard on the knot.

14. Triple knot all the lace up to your pins, then move them up the same distance, pin in again and repeat the triple knots.

15. Comb through, damp them, and cut out the roots. (*See* 'Cutting Out the Roots' in Example 1.)

16. Fill in the remaining lace with single knots and two hairs till the wig is complete. Comb it all through and damp it for the density check before trimming the style.

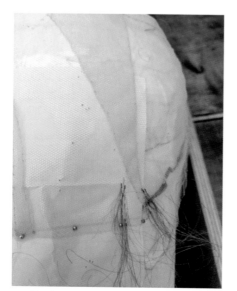

Triple knotting the nape examples.

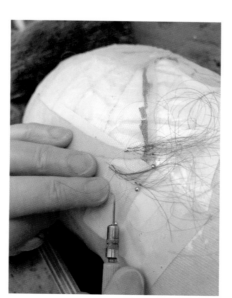

Over the next lace bar.

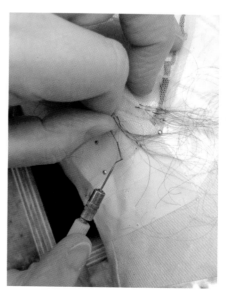

Double knot.

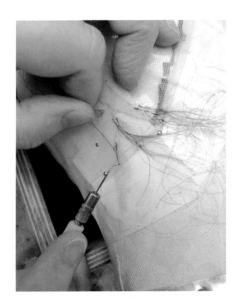

Triple knot hook.

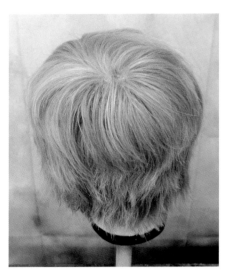

Styled wig from the back.

Triple knot pull through.

CUTTING THE WIG

The hair will be 3cm long at its shortest and 5cm at its longest, cut in feathers. Do this by holding the hair with your comb at right angles to the wig and chopping into the lengths with the points of your scissors.

DRESSING THE WIG

Comb through the wet wig out from the crown and on to the face with a break, down at the sides in front of the ears, down the back from the crown. Use your tail comb to flick edges to give a little movement. The longer hair in each feather will give a softer edge to the front and nape, rather than the modern clippered look.

Styled Henry VIII wig and facial hair.

EXAMPLE 3: THIRD TUDOR MAN

Third Tudor Man: *Young Man Among Roses* by Nicholas Hilliard.

This wig is for one of the many instances we mentioned earlier when a girl disguises herself as a boy. When Rosalind cuts her own hair to disguise

NOTES

Medium length, permed hair. Girl to boy (in Shakespeare's day, boy to girl to boy) for Rosalind as Ganymede in *As You Like It*. Style is a reflection of the late Tudor romantic, nostalgic view of life in the Greenwood. A poetic, artful disarray referenced in a miniature of a young man relaxing under a flowering bush. Quick change!

herself as Ganymede, to look natural and unstyled, the hair lies in curled layers to the shoulders.

This wig goes on as part of a quick change out of Rosalind's court costume and hairstyle. Shakespeare has written some lines, Act 2 scenes 1, 2 and 3, to allow for this, but it is still quick!

- Her own hair can be prepared before the show to keep a tight, flat head shape which will securely hold under both wigs.
- This wig will be lace-fronted, fully knotted with real hair that has been permed before knotting to give a gentle, tousled effect. If permed when the wig is finished, it will look too styled for the forest.

If your actor has darker skin, this makes a lovely short and curly wig with darker lace and coiled hair.

Black Oberried Altarpiece (left wing panel) *The Adoration of the Magi* by Hans Holbein the Younger.

- Daily roller setting and heat drying will damage the hair, but curled hair can be damp set in pin curls if required and simply left in a warm place.
- This foundation is going to fit over hair that has been wrapped flat on the top of the head but is quite full where it has been spread over and below the occipital bone.

Making the Hat Band Foundation

We are going to use a 'hat band' or 'circumference band' foundation. The nape piece is slightly shaped in a curve at the centre of the nape, shorter in the middle of the nape and sloping slightly down towards the ear to nape line.

The nape piece itself will continue up from the ear to ear point, over the top of the head. To avoid a seam on the front of the wig, the lace will have a seam centre back.

1. To cut out the band of lace (N1) it is necessary to make a pattern from the shell.
2. Draw the outline of the band on half the shell, then cover it with cling film or a polythene bag. Mark the centre

Aaron and Tamora in *Titus Andronicus*.

A short, curled wig with brown lace and 3A hair.

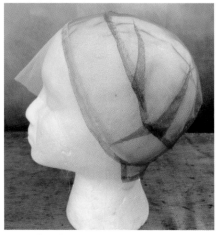

Finished hat-band foundation.

Cutting out the hat-band lace (left side).

Cutting out the hat-band lace (right side).

front CF, centre nape CN and ear CE.

3. Sticky tape the cling film for strength, then trace the outline with a marker pen and tape over that.
4. Remove the pattern from the block and cut off the excess film up to the marker pen line.
5. Measure the length of the pattern and lay it on a folded piece of foundation net the right size. The

centre front line, CF, is on the fold. The lace lines are vertical from the inner position of the centre front fold, down to the centre of the over-ear curve (CE).

6. Add 1.5cm all round for seam allowance before you cut.
7. Lay the net on the block, with the fold centre front, 4cm behind the hairline and the cut edge upright in the centre back. Pin it. It is now inside out.
8. Fold the nape up 0.5cm, then again 1cm to make a tidy seam, pin and whip it along the sides and back of the nape and over the ear arches (CE), rounding off the corners at the side of the nape.
9. Remove N1 from the block and turn it so the seams sit against the block. The centre nape point (CN) should sit on the hairline of the nape, the sides slightly outside the hairline. Pin it securely. The inner edge can be folded up and whipped.
10. The crown piece (N2) will be a rectangle the size of the ear to ear measurement on the front edge and the length of the front to nape

measurement on the other, following the lace lines, which will go from front to back; cut this out.

11. Sit the crown piece on the top of the head, slightly overlapping N1 all round, with the lines going from front to nape. Pin it. Work round the front edge keeping the lace flat, then at the sides and back gather the excess lace into tucks.
12. Pin and whip the tacks over a doofer.

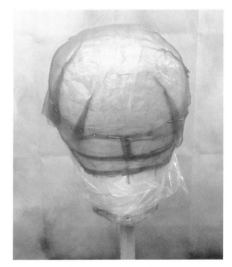

Back of crown piece.

Crown piece attached, tucked and ready to whip.

Front of crown piece is smooth with no seams.

13. Trim off the excess lace from N2 leaving 1cm to fold under over the whipped inside edge of N1. Whip this seam in two rows.
14. Take a piece of front lace long enough to cover the hairline all round, with the lines going from side to side. Fold, mark, and centre it on the foundation, lines going from side to side and a pin on the centre line, smooth down and pin, 5cm in front of the hairline. Smooth the front lace back and pin it over N2.
15. Smooth the sides back and pin over N2. Make small tucks to distribute the excess lace, pin and whip them over a doofer.
16. Trim the lace to leave a 1cm overlap with N2 and fold this under to make a seam. Pin and whip this.
17. Remove the pins in front of the hairline on the front lace and run in a cotton line.

Knotting the Young Man's Wig

This will be knotted in the same way as the First Tudor Man, coming forward in a fringe from a cross-knotted centre break, using 15cm pre-curled hair in shades of brown.

Cutting the Wig

This may not be necessary, as the knotting will have reduced the length.

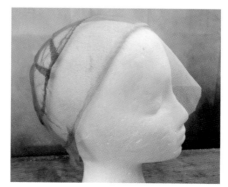
Elastic at the nape to tighten.

The knotting itself will have resulted in a 12cm layered look, which the curls will have reduced by a quarter.

Extras

Add an elastic inside each ear to nape side, to tighten it. As we have made that area slightly larger than the shell, it will still hide all the hair.

Add a clip comb inside the centre front of the wig for a quick fix; it will make putting the wig on in the quick change easier.

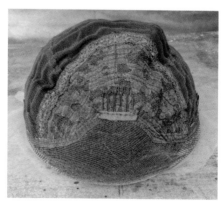
Combs at front and sides to avoid glue for quick change.

Styling the Wig

1. After knotting and checking for density, adding the elastic and clip combs, block up the wig and comb through.
2. Spray the wig with water and comb again with a large toothed comb.
3. Scrunch small sections of the hair in your hands to encourage the curl.
4. Leave to dry naturally.

Third Tudor Man's wig for Rosalind as a young man.

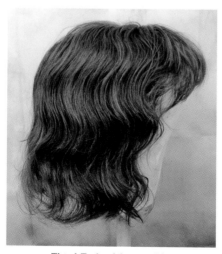
Third Tudor Man profile.

Making Sixteenth-Century Female Wigs and Dressing

5

EXAMPLE 1: FIRST TUDOR WOMAN

In many plays, plentiful wigs may be required to highlight the different roles. In our example here, *A Midsummer Night's Dream*, there are wigs to show differences between the court and the commoners, the actors' initial characters and their play-within-the-play roles, and the fairies and humans. The budget may require that this large stock of wigs be made quickly and cheaply.

Therefore, the wig is to be bought in as a pre-made, knotted lace-front wig in synthetic fibre, to look more obviously fake as part of a costume. There are a wide range of synthetic wigs available online and so long as it has a lace front you cannot go too wrong. Look for reviews and photos from their other clients. Avoid companies who are using stolen photographs – you will soon start to recognize them.

Fibre is cheap but has consequences for our planet. Wig makers traditionally use it sparingly and re-furbish and re-use it as much as any other of our materials. With more time, you could make a foundation and sew unravelled hemp

Thisbe with long, loose curls by Nicolaus Knüpfer, *Pyrame et Thisbé*.

rope, or flax, to a base, even the head of a cotton mop can be utilized. These give an even more obvious and therefore humorous appearance.

Buying in Wigs

Anyone can buy a ready-made wig, but will it arrive on time? Is it the right colour and length? Will it even fit the actor? These questions and your expertise are the reason you have been delegated to solve the problem. The preparation time for a new play is sometimes short, you

Pre-bought synthetic wigs and a custom pink beehive.

NOTES

The male actor playing Flute the Bellows Mender in *A Midsummer Night's Dream*, dresses up as Thisbe, a young lady, for a play-within-the-play.

LEFT: Female beehive in black rolls styled for Titania.

may only have two or three weeks. On the plus side, you could order far more than needed and return the unsuitable options.

Record keeping. Whenever you buy hair or wigs, keep a record. Who sold it to you? How long did it take to arrive? Are they local? What did you think of the wig? To what temperature is that fibre heat resistant? What was the exact style and colour code so you can re-order quickly?

Brick and mortar shops. You can save time but pay a little more to buy from a shop where you can see the wig at first hand rather than buying more cheaply online.

Ready-made wig foundations. These vary enormously, from simple elastic caps of caul net, with hard fronts, to good lace foundations with knotted fronts. Take a picture of the inside as well as the outside of any wig you buy.

Lace fronts – It is always better to pay more for a knotted and lace-fronted wig, as they are more easily adapted and longer lasting.

Front lace. Colours and denier vary between suppliers. Bleaching, dyeing and replacing front lace are all options to consider.

Types of fibre. The choice of fibre is another challenge. Hair has a cuticle resembling the scales on a snake. This cuticle is easily damaged by rough handling or chemicals, especially if wet. Damage will remove the shine and it is difficult to restore.

- Straighter fibre is the shiniest and generally a thicker, weightier fibre is used for straight wigs, making adaptions difficult.
- Very curly wigs are usually of a thinner and lighter-weight fibre, but difficult to smooth successfully to change the style.
- Long plastic hair may be too heavy to wear comfortably and requires thinning.

Different types of synthetic hair.

Using Heat on Synthetic Hair

Ensure you have checked this specific wig's manufacturer's advice on the maximum hair temperature before using curlers with heated tongs or straighteners. With all synthetic fibres, you can use a handheld fabric steamer to warm the hair around rollers but this will leave the hair wet. If you are able to afford a hooded hairdryer or oven, use rollers on sprayed-damp hair and leave to dry. If not, leaving it blocked on a towel-covered radiator or windowsill will help speed the drying process.

Thinning your Wig

The most likely candidate for Thisbe is a wig that has some wave in it and is the right length and colour. Cutting out alternate layers of weft will reduce the weight but leave bare patches. Thinning the weft by working carefully through the wig cutting 0.5cm out of the weft at the root every 4cm with scissors, or using thinning scissors may be less obvious but is time consuming. Whichever method you choose, save the fibre and keep it to re-use.

Removing Shine from a Synthetic Wig

There are recipes to purposefully remove the shine from plastic hair, such as soaking with alcohol, vinegar or fabric softener, but the only sure way is abrasion, damaging the smooth plastic surface of the fibre. Rubbing with a baking soda paste, backcombing or dressing in tight rollers are the methods employed, but the best solution is to find a wig that is not too shiny to start with.

Changing the Colour of Fibre

One of the plus points of plastic hair is the huge variety of colours it offers us. The wigs are available with dark roots, streaks and ombre effects. You can also buy in hairpieces of the required colour, cut out the weft and sew it into a wig or

Dyeing synthetic fibre with acrylic dye – follow instructions.

knot in the new colour. Sprays, grease or gel products can be used for temporary colours.

Dyeing of any sort will only make the fibre darker. Streaks and roots can be achieved with a marker pen. Rarely, you may want to dye the fibre wig itself. The base of the wig will take dye differently from the fibre. As usual, results vary and you must do test samples, both for the quantity of dye powder to use, the length of time it will take to effect change, and the effect of higher temperatures on the fibre.

We will cover two methods for dyeing the wig below. There are other ways, but these have led to our most successful results.

In all cases, use a well-ventilated space with good light, access to water and the means to heat it, with wipe-clean surfaces and an uncluttered floor. As a freelance worker, this means your workroom, kitchen or bathroom. Consider whether you want to take the risk of staining your work surfaces or whether you should cover them with bin liners or cling film for smaller pieces before you start.

The door must close to keep out children, pets or unexpected visitors.

Method 1: Polyester fabric dye

Any polyester dye will work to stain the fibres. iDye Poly is the safest dye as the powder comes in a soluble packet. With other types, the fibre may need more dye powder than the manufacturer recommends because you are not able to boil the fibre up to the suggested temperature without damage. The colour may be reached within about ten minutes, far less time than they suggest, leaving it in a dye bath longer will not deepen the colour and may damage it more.

PRO TIP

These pans are expensive to buy but can be bought cheaply in charity shops. When you are looking, visualize a wig block immersed in it – if it would fit, that will be the right size.

TOOLS:

- Personal protection for yourself: a waterproof apron, face mask and eye-shield, rubber gloves and waterproof, undyeable boots or shoes. Pin your hair off your face, otherwise you will stain your face and it might get into your eyes.
- The notes you made from the test, a kitchen timer and jam thermometer.
- Two large, deep pans that may become stained and unusable for cooking. Large enough to hold the whole wig in water at once and still allow the fibres to move.
- A deep sieve or wired fishing net that can sit over the large pan, allowing the wig to be lowered into the hot water, but not touch the bottom of the pan. Without this support, the wig will drop to the bottom of the pan and be in contact with the hottest part, possibly suffering heat damage.
- A washing-up bowl, which might become stained.
- A pair of laundry tongs.
- Some clean towels you are ready to sacrifice.
- A mixing bowl with silicone lid and stainless steel straw (or chopstick) to mix the dye, the dye powder and measure.
- A camping type of washing line that you can fix up over the sink, and clips to hold the wig to it.
- Laundry liquid and fabric softener.
- Wig block covered in cling film, wig stand, blocking pins, large comb.

Polyester fabric dye.

METHOD 1:

1. Block up and comb through the wig. Unblock it. There may be combs inside the wig; you can remove them to dye it, then re-instate them in better places for the style (if desired) before you start to dress the wig.
2. Half-fill the washing-up bowl with lukewarm water and a little laundry liquid. Add the wig and wash it gently, not tangling the fibres. This is to remove any coating there may be on the fibres. Remove wig, empty bowl and refill with clean, warm water to rinse the wig thoroughly. Check the temperature. Hand-hot water will work until you are ready.
3. Open the window. Mix up the dye in a bowl with warm water to make a runny consistency. This is rather like mixing bleach with peroxide: beware of inhaling powder or fumes. A

PRO TIP

The iPoly dye comes in a soluble packet that goes straight in the pot, a safer choice.

silicone cover over the bowl with a small slit for a metal straw or chopstick to stir with is one way of mixing them together safely.

4. Half-fill one of the pans with water, take it to the stove and bring up the temperature. Do not let it boil. Add the dye mixture or packet to the pan and blend. Half-fill the second pan with water and put on the stove next to the first one.

Warm water prepared in kettle and cold stove.

5. Turn on your timer.
6. Empty the clean water from the washing-up bowl and use it to carry the wet wig to the dye pan. Set your sieve on top and lay the wig in it. Using the laundry tongs, swirl the wig in the dye to be evenly coated, stay with it to keep it moving gently for even coverage.

7. Heat the clean water in the second pan but only until hand hot, then turn off the heat.
8. When your timer goes, or at the most after ten minutes, test a sample of fibre by rinsing it in the second pan. When the colour is right, turn off the heat, lift the wig with the sieve and immerse it in the warm water in the second pan.
9. Bring the washing-up bowl to the stove and pick up the wig with the tongs and drop it in. Take the bowl to

Check on the colour.

Use tongs to dip.

Strain and wash.

Sky blue from half a packet of Tropical Green.

the sink and rinse the wig in clean water until the water runs clear. Wash the wig with a little laundry liquid and clean water. Rinse again and add fabric softener to the water.
10. Lift the wig and pin it to the clothes line above the sink to drip. Clear up the mess. Take your wig stand and blocking tools back to the wig room. Close the window.
11. Use the towels to pat the wig dry and pin it back up. If any dye has come off on the towels you will need to repeat the washing and rinsing.
12. When the wig is dry, replace any combs and block it up as normal. Allow it to dry and then check the colour. If it is not dark enough, repeat the dyeing process for a further ten minutes. Remember it can only go darker, not lighter.

Method 2: Using Alcohol to Dye a Synthetic Wig

It is possible to work with cooler water and avoid the stove, making this a quicker option.

Using alcohol and marker pens to dye hair.

TOOLS:

- PPE as in Method 1.
- A white or lightest blonde lace-front wig in the correct length, cut and texture. This is so you can be sure of the exact result you are getting. Feel free, of course, to experiment if you have a wig close to the correct shade.
- A selection of appropriately coloured alcohol-based marker pens. Just one will create a pastel colour, so you may need several to get an intense colour.
- 1 litre of 70 per cent rubbing alcohol.
- 2 litre empty plastic bottle.
- Scissors, box cutter or craft knife.
- Pliers.
- 1 litre metal or glass bowl.
- Funnel.
- Flat tinting brush(es) in appropriate widths.
- Sectioning clips and butterfly clips if required.
- Plastic box or bucket big enough to fit a wig block inside.
- Clean hairdressing towels.
- Laundry tongs, large kitchen tongs or a spaghetti server.
- Plastic sheets, bin liners and so on to protect surfaces.

METHOD 2:

1. Protect yourself and your surfaces as in Method 1.
2. Wash the wig as in Method 1.
3. You will be using the empty plastic bottle to mix the rubbing alcohol with the marker pens' interior inkwells. Undo the cap of your plastic bottle and pour in enough alcohol to ensure the inkwells will be covered. More alcohol to dye creates a lighter colour but it is essential that you have plenty to soak the wig. Put the cap back on.
4. Uncap the marker pens and use the pliers to pull off the inkwell cap and the nib. Put the nib on a covered surface. Use the pliers to extract the inkwells. Undo the bottle cap and pop in the nibs now before they dry and replace the bottle cap so that the alcohol does not evaporate.
5. Over the bowl to catch any dripping ink, use your scissors or knife to slit open the plastic sheath of the inkwell and remove the fibrous inner lining.
6. Open the bottle cap and drop the fibrous inkwell into the rubbing alcohol. Replace the cap and swirl, swish and agitate with a chopstick. The darker the colour, the brighter the shade on the wig will be. You may want to leave it to allow the alcohol to fully absorb the dye. Keep an eye on it.
7. Take a small section of the synthetic hair from where it won't be missed on the wig if you are forced to cut it out. The middle of the centre back and over the ears are often bulky on pre-bought wigs.
8. Pour the alcohol-dye into the bowl using your chopstick to stop the bits

---

PRO TIP

It would be easiest to simply chop a small lock of hair from one area where it won't be needed. If this isn't achievable, back comb a section four times, pull together the random strands remaining in your hand and cut this lock off. This technique makes the loss less visible once combed out.

---

of inkwell from leaving the bottle. Begin to experiment with the alcohol-based dye on your sample strand. You may need to use the funnel to return the dye to the (now empty) bottle and add further inkwells to add depth or change the colour.

9. Once you have the perfect shade, prepare the wig with clips or grips to tackle the underneath first. This way if something terrible happens with the colour, it will be hidden from the top.
10. Apply the colour. Use the bucket or plastic box so you have room for the entire wig, plus your arms.

Full coverage – Clip the wig by its front lace to tongs or chopsticks to stop it from reaching the dye, but allowing all the other hair to soak, getting the richest colour. Pour some of the dye back into your small bowl and quickly apply it with your tinting brushes to ensure the hair closest to the front lace is also receiving plentiful coverage.

Streaks or roots – Apply the dye with the tinting brush and smaller bowl as appropriate.

Dip-dyeing – This can create a lovely ombre effect if you repeatedly

Acrylic dye in pink, marker pen in blue.

dunk it, allowing the ends to pick up most colour.

11. Keep an eye on the wig's colour. When it looks correct, rinse and wash your wig as in Method 1, dry, and check the colour. If it needs more colour, repeat the dyeing process. Remember it can only go darker.

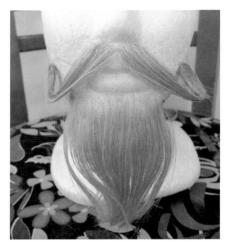

Mixing different pink synthetics to create a more interesting depth of colour.

Mixing blue and green to get turquoise.

Mixing Hair Colours

Experiment with creating precise and interesting looks by blending or mixing your synthetic colours to get a more custom effect. This avoids the all-one-colour look, which can be distractingly unnatural.

DRESSING THE WIG

Thisbe is a young woman, meeting her lover. Her hair will be mostly down, from a centre break, held back from her face at the sides. As the story of Pyramus and Thisbe is taken from the works of the Roman poet Ovid, we will dress the wig in snaky ringlets to give it a classical feel.

TOOLS:
- Large clips to hold the hair out of the way.
- Long blue bendy rollers, which are tubes of foam about 20cm long with a wire core.
- A tail comb.
- Hair grips.
- Big pins.
- Hand-held steamer.
- Kitchen tongs to hold the roller.

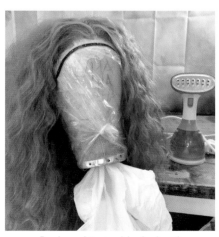

Pre-bought wig, blocked with waterproofing to stand, galloon on front lace.

METHOD:
1. Block the wig as usual and comb through. We will start the set from the nape and work forward.
2. If you start from on top, after you wind each roller, bend it up or it will be in the way as you work the underneath rows.
3. Put on a waterproof apron and lay a towel on the floor around the wig stand. We are going to steam the wig and there will be drips.
4. Section off the nape of the wig with your tail comb and pin the rest up. Take a piece of fibre from an area the width of the bendy and pull it down 3cm. This dragging will allow the ringlets to hang rather than giving width.
5. Hold and twist from the root end, winding it round the roller, spiral twisting as you go.

PRO TIP

This will make a crisp lift to each wave in the snaky ringlets. Without the twist it would just be a ringlet and seem more Victorian in style.

Twist the hair as you wrap it around the yellow bendy to create ringlets.

6. Use a hairgrip to hold the ends of fibre in place. Use a large pin to hold the bendy roller to the wig at the root.

7. Put your wig in your wig oven to heat the roller set. This is the most convenient, least messy method. *See instruction 9 if this applies to you.*

OR

Set up your steamer and begin to work on each bendy roller as you complete it. This ensures each one is thoroughly warmed. Use kitchen tongs to hold the roller, but do not steam your hands. Hold the steamer a couple of inches away then steam for twenty seconds on each section of the roller. Adjust your wig stand so the angle of the roller allows you to steam under and over it.

8. Work up the wig, putting all the fibre in the bendies and steaming them as you go.

If a wig is set in perm rollers, as our Titania will be, you can fill a bowl with very hot water and, holding the wig by the nape of the block, plunge it in for a few seconds, followed by a dowsing with cold water.

Heat is the constant factor in fibre setting, how much heat is the unknown – always do a test on the fibre with your chosen method.

9. Whichever method you choose, let the fibre cool before you remove the rollers. If steamed, pat it dry, unblock the wig and lay it flat on a towel for the inside to dry out before you re-block it to dress.

Dress the Style

In the case of Thisbe's wig, this is a simple dressing.

1. Use your fingers to separate some of the snaky pieces. Take a section from in front of each ear and twist them back to below the crown where they will meet and be held with a small rubber band.

2. Tie a ribbon over this to look as if that is what is holding the hair back.

3. Pull a little fibre from the sideburns to hang down in a ringlet in front of the ears. This will hide the hairpins holding the sides of the wig to the cap underneath. Cut a few baby hairs to come over the lace and hide it.

Simply dressed Thisbe with gold ribbon.

EXAMPLE 2: SECOND TUDOR WOMAN

These are not typically leading characters, but all are essential to the plot; powerful women, brave and intelligent. The countess in *All's Well That Ends Well* or Paulina in *The*

Marie de' Medici (1575–1642) by Peter Paul Rubens, similar to Second Tudor Woman.

NOTES

The wig should be a natural grey with a centre parting with high, padded crescents and a bun. Will mostly be worn under a cap or French hood.

Winter's Tale or the Duchess of York in *Richard III*.

- A full-lace, knotted wig with set-in parting and selvedge nape to match the actor's skin tone will be used. The nape will have frillies around the edge.

- Use toupee clips in the nape to hold it closed and a few perimeter curls to soften the edges.

- Cover the bun with a hair net as it will not need to be re-dressed every time, and a lace cap will be worn.

- To give status, the front hair is raised, taken back from a centre parting over pads.

Up-Do Foundations

When the nape hair is dressed up there will be less difficulty with hiding seams, therefore less hair need be used. A natural looking nape is essential if the back of the wig is seen. The design shows our lady in a French hood over a cap, but in a more domestic scene of the play the hood may be removed. Our wig is more useful if it is adaptable and justifies the cost of materials and time with its versatility. Making this will be covered in Chapter 8.

Padding

SYNTHETIC HAIR PADS AND DOUGHNUTS
For hygienic reasons, the commercial synthetic pads are preferable. They can be washed and dried easily and re-used. Supplied in bun rings, sausages and crescents, with clips and nets, they can also be taken apart and re-shaped to suit the project.

CREPE HAIR
There are two similar items:
A: Crepe hair. This is hair that has been damped, tightly plaited as one tresse with two strings, and boiled or baked in the wig oven to permanently curl it. The curl or wave can be adjusted with the thickness of the hair tresse and that of the string you use.

Creping long hair produces an Afro curl and that is the most frequent use today, an alternative to the chopstick perm. It is used for laying false beards and moustaches directly on the actor's skin, with glue. This has become less common with the availability of extra fine laces, but the technique is still used by skilled make-up artists to disguise the edges of lace in wigs and facial.

Crepe hair can be glued directly on a chin block instead to make a beard or moustache. After it has dried and been cut and dressed it must be sprayed with lacquer or a fixing spray. Remove it from the chin block by gently feeding acetone under the hair with a cotton bud to dissolve the glue enough to lift off while retaining the beard shape.

The same procedure can make a wig. This is a bit messy, but once mastered produces single-use postiche much more quickly than knotting.
B: Crepe wool. This is wool plaited with strings and boiled or baked in the same way as crepe hair. When pulled from the strings it can be fanned out to produce a filler for buns and mounds, making a cheap pad. The wool can be any colour to suit the wig and the pad can be any size, wrapped in a hairnet to keep the required shape; it has long been a wig dresser's staple.

These pads (sometimes called 'rats' – you'll know why when one slips out of the bag and lurks in the cupboard) are removed when the wig is washed, and it is easy to forget that they need to be cleaned as well. Crepe hair and crepe wool are both best dry-cleaned with acetone.

Grey Hair

Grey hair is described in terms of percentages of white hair to the original colour, for example a white wig could be 100 per cent grey. White hair or fibre on stage concentrates the light and produces a halo effect, looking more like a dandelion clock than hair, and is rarely requested by designers. More often they will request white streaks in a wig that is 50 per cent grey on top and 25 per cent

> **PRO TIP**
> Hair is valued by texture, colour and length. Long, white hair is the most expensive to buy. Using white fibre in part of the wig will keep costs down. If this were an eighteenth-century style you might prefer to use yak hair for body.

Various real and synthetic white and grey wigs.

L–R: mohair, belly yak, tail yak and larger tail yak.

grey at the nape, so this is what we will be building.

Use the shortest possible length of hair to create this style and add extra to the bun with fibre padding or a switch, approx. 30cm hair, 250g: that is 100g white, plus 50g each of the three base colours to mix.

Mixing Hair

This should be done in the hand with small quantities of hair and a large comb. Hair is easily stretched by rough handling, losing all elasticity instantly and forever.

1. Lay your colours on a mat or hairbrushes, untied, and uncovered. Roots to the right.
2. Take up a tresse of each colour by the roots and hold them together in one hand, with your thumb on top and

the comb in your dominant hand, comb through.

3. Divide the hank in three and let the middle third drop down between the forefinger and the middle finger. Flip the colours over each other in the beginning of a plait.
4. Do three plaits, then move your grip a quarter of the way down the hank, hold securely, and comb through the root end.
5. Now move your grip back to the root end and comb through the lengths. After a couple of repeats you will have mixed it all.

If you pull too hard at a tangle, the comb will break before the hair can be stretched.

The Foundation

TOOLS:
- One metre of grey or a flesh colour appropriate for the actor in Terylene, soft, 30 denier foundation net, full width with selvedge edge.
- One 50cm length of front lace, 15 or 20 denier in a flesh colour suited to your actor.

METHOD:
1. Set your hair in the mats and have your equipment to hand.
2. Copy the shell on to the wig block and mark up your centre lines as usual.
3. Take the ear to nape and across nape measurements and double them. Cut a selvedge edge this length from

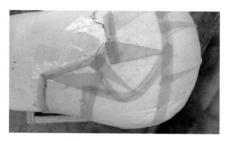

Pleats over the ears.

your foundation lace that is 7cm wide.

4. Start from the front of the ear position and pin your selvedge strip all around and just below the nape line. Pleat it over the ears to make the curve and fold it at the corners.
5. Whip these pleats and folds (*see* N1 on the four-piece foundation). Fold 0.5cm of the upper edge of N1 towards you, as a seam to lie under the N2, pin and whip it. This edge is non-run and will replace the three layers in the bottom seam of the wig foundation with the equivalent of a single layer of lace.
6. Measure the distance from the nape up to 10cm above the ear points. For the other measurement you will use the temple to temple distance from the actor's notes. (This piece of lace will cover the area covered by N2 in the first foundation.)
7. Cut out the lace and set it on the block with dominant lines from front to nape along the centre line, the bottom edge overlapping N1 by 2cm.
8. Put several pins in along the front-to-nape line to hold it still while you work and keep the lace lines perpendicular.
9. Smooth each side towards the front and pin them. Go down to the centre of the nape and pin the lace down. Work your way around the upper edge of N1 pinning the lace down. It is better to have tucks centre back than at the sides as there will be

more hair there to hide the tucks.

10. When it is all pinned and evenly distributed, whip the tucks over your doofer.

11. Trim the lower edge of the lace to an even 1.5cm overlap.

12. Fold the lace under by 0.5cm to make the seam, pin it and whip it in two lines.

13. Go to the top horizontal edge of N2 and fold it towards you, making a seam 0.5cm deep. Pin and whip this once.

14. The third piece of lace (N3) will lie over the top of the head with dominant lines from front to nape. This piece of lace will sit 3cm behind the front edge of the wig and overlap N2 by 1.5cm. Cut it out and pin it down along the centre line from front to back.

15. Smooth the top front of the lace to the block and tuck the excess lace at the sides where it meets N1 and pin it. Tuck and pin the centre back section. Whip down the tucks over your doofer.

16. Trim around the bottom edge to leave a 1cm overlap with N2, fold 0.5cm of this under to be a seam, pin and whip two rows. This piece of lace (N3) will hold the centre parting cut-out.

17. Make a cut in N3 along the centre line of the block for 8cm. At the crown end, make a small cut of 0.5cm on each side. Fold the two side wings up and away along the length of the cut at an angle, leaving at least a 6cm gap at the front edge.

18. Fold their outer edges under by a few millimetres, pin and whip down.

19. Fold up the tab at the crown end and pin the edge under by a few millimetres. Take your whipping all the way around from one side of the cut to the other; at the end of the cut, continue to whip to strengthen the edge of cut lace where there is

nothing to fold.

20. Check that this lace sits 3cm away from the cotton line on the front edge.

21. Fold up 0.5cm and whip it down.

22. Take up your front lace piece and lay it on the hairline of the block, centre it and smooth the lace back over the cut in the under lace and beyond by at least 2cm to make the seam.

23. Keep the front lace over the cut-out area flat with your hand and pin it. Smooth the centre front of the lace down the block and pin it.

24. Take each side of the front lace and arrange them symmetrically, taking tucks as needed but not on the hairline itself or the parting. Pin and whip the tucks.

25. Pin and whip the edges of the parting. Cut where they meet the front lace.

26. Pin the front lace over the edge of the under laces all round. Leave 1cm for seam allowance and cut off the excess.

27. Fold the front lace down onto the under lace to make a 0.5cm seam, pin and whip.

28. Remove the foundation from the block and check that all the inside seams and tucks have been

whipped.

29. Sew in small clip combs, open teeth ends up to crown, bar against the net, either side of the nape, inside the foundation. These will hold the nape of the wig close to the head.

30. Re-block the wig foundation and prepare to knot.

Knotting the Grey Wig

1. Begin with the parting, starting at a point furthest from the front edge, at the centre point of the parting, on the centre line of the block.

2. Your knots will be single hairs in every hole, reversed, so as you knot the hair will lie towards the face at an angle of 45 degrees. Fill in every hole for 1cm each side of the parting until you reach 2cm from the front edge. Comb this hair and make it into a pin curl to keep it out of the way.

3. The front edge: single hairs in alternate holes from two holes in front of the cotton line to five holes behind. They will lie back from the face, out from the parting mark at a 45-degree angle, like the parting. At each side the knots will be angled down towards the ears.

4. Now turn your block to begin reverse

Front lace with parting (not blocked up).

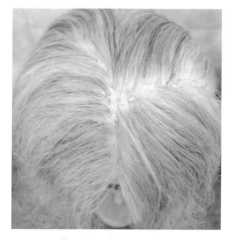

Knotting the grey wig.

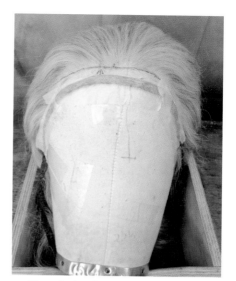

Knot the hairline first, single knots.

knotting the rest of the front lace, two hairs in alternate holes.

5. At this point, release all the hair and comb it back as it will be styled; thickness may be an issue. Is there enough coverage in front of those seams? If not, add more hair. The other issue is the colour: are your streaks reading or do they need emphasizing? Again, add more hair to correct.

6. Comb through and pin curl away the front and parting hair before you start the nape. As the wig will be styled up, the sides of the nape will be reverse knotted – knotted outwards and down.

7. Single hairs in alternate holes all around the edge for the first two holes are a semblance of front edge. Nothing draws the eye as 'wiggie'

PRO TIP

Adjust as you go, thickening through is agony. Remember to double knot on seams.

like a thick nape line.

8. Knot two or three hairs in alternate holes for the rest of the wig. Pause to check that your seams are hidden and that your nape is fractionally darker than your top, and streaky.

Dressing the Second Tudor Woman's Grey Wig

TOOLS:
- Large toothed comb.
- Tail combs.
- Rollers.
- Pins.
- Clips.
- Water spray.
- Micropore tape.
- Galloon.

METHOD:
1. Bring out your roller plan for this wig and the design you are working to. Be prepared to adjust the plan to suit the styles you need in future.
2. This set will entail some rollers sitting on the front lace. Protect it by laying some micropore tape over the small pins and galloon you have

Lots of volume before a brush through and a centre parting.

Separate at the parting and ear to ear.

used to block up.

3. Put the block on the stand, comb through with a large comb, perhaps Black Diamond by DUPONT giant waver 215mm, or a handle rake 220mm, and spray lightly with water.

4. Check again once it has dried whether there are any thin patches, awkward streaks or obvious seams, especially around the nape and parting, and make corrections.

5. Begin with the front section either side of the parting. Use your tail comb to section off all the hair in front of the ear-to-ear line and comb it forward, as if on to the face and clip it.

PRO TIP

You will notice that I say comb, rather than brush. Brushes are speedy de-tanglers, good on human heads, but they add volume and static to hair – neither are needed at this point.

Front view of grey roller set.

Side view of grey roller set.

Getting the pads in position.

6. Damp the hair lightly as you work on each section.
7. Lift the remaining parting hair on one side with your tail comb and roller it with 18mm metal or flock rollers. Sit each roller on its base rather than dragging it to get lift and wave all over the wig.
8. Use your tail comb to keep your ends straight and hold the roller in place with a large pin.
9. Make two rows of rollers in a semi-circle around the wig, with the hair going down.
10. Section off the sides of the nape and

Rear view of grey roller set.

clip them. Roller the centre back hair to go up towards the crown.
11. The hair on each side of the nape will be rolled in towards these centre back rollers, parallel to the sides of the nape itself.
12. Feel at the edges of the nape for short root hairs that can be eased out of their roller and pin curled down on to the neck to soften the edge, a version of baby hairs sometimes used on wig fronts. Slightly longer hairs wound around a hairpin make 'frillies', an optional extra.
13. Return to the front. This hair will go over pads to make it look fuller, so use the same size rollers but over-extend them, so they are sitting in front of their base section, on the front of the wig. The resulting flat area is where the pads will sit.
14. Feel the roller in front of the ears for baby hairs that can be eased out and pin curled for softness.

Styling the Wig

TOOLS:
• Combs.
• Small elastic bands.
• Grips.
• Pins.

• Pads of grey crepe hair in hair nets.
• Commercial hair pads.
• An extra switch for the bun.
• A hair net.
• Hairspray/lacquer.

METHOD:
1. When the wig has dried and cooled and the rollers and pin curls have been removed, part the hair at a diagonal from the ears to the crown. Pull the front hair forward and clip.
2. Comb through the nape hair. Divide the hair into three sections and take each up to the crown. Use small elastics to hold them.
3. Fold the hair into a bun over a pad of matching fibre, crepe hair or crepe wool or plastic fibre for bulk. A plastic bun-ring would be too much for this style. The bun should sit level with the top of the head. Pin it with hooked fine hairpins and cover with a fine net.
4. Separate the front hair vertically on each side so two thirds lies forwards on to the face and the rest is taken into pin curls on each side of the parting, which will support the pad.

Front hair over pads and pinned.

Wrapping the two curls together.

Final dressing.

5. Set each pad in place with fine hooked hairpins to hold it, or tack it in with a curved needle, being careful either way not to attach the pad to the wig block. Or you can sew small clip combs to each pad and use these to hold them to the wig.

6. Take the hair on each side of the front and backcomb it slightly along

Rear of grey up-do.

the full length of hair. Smooth the front and outer edges, then arrange these two hanks to make crescent shapes on either side over the pads. When they match, pin their ends into the foundation and spray with lacquer.

7. The back will not be seen so a neat chignon will do the trick.
   - Divide the nape horizontally.
   - Roll the top and bottom sections into two curls.
   - Wrap the two curls around each other at the occipital bone.
   - Pin securely.
   - Add the French hood and veil for the final touch.

Horizontal split with two curls.

EXAMPLE 3: THIRD TUDOR WOMAN – PERIWIG 1

The large, hard-fronted wigs worn by Queen Elizabeth I in the late Tudor period were referred to as 'periwigs' in The Great Wardrobe Accounts. There is also mention of a periwig in the play *The Two Gentlemen of Verona*, one of Shakespeare's earliest plays, written possibly in 1594 or 1595.

- The wig for Titania could be hard fronted to facilitate the quick changes, or have a lace front, which of itself helps to keep the wig securely on the head. Our version will be hard fronted.
- We will use 4C naturally curly hair to suit the actor's skin tone. The Tudor curls can be achieved with fibre, which will hold the curl successfully with little maintenance, or pre-curled hair.
- We will use Elizabeth I's appearance in her last painting for reference.

Queen Elizabeth I, *The Ditchley Portrait* by Marcus Gheeraerts the Younger.

NOTES

This will be Titania, Queen of the Fairies. The play is *A Midsummer Night's Dream*. Tudors believed in fairies as human-sized entities. The actor has two parts, also taking the role of Hippolyta, Queen of the Amazons, whose wedding celebrations round off the play. Both are strong, powerful leaders – Titania taking reference from Queen Elizabeth I. To suit her role as Amazonian queen, our actor has dark skin. We want fairyland extravagance and a headdress to mark this character as distinct from Hippolyta. There will be a quick change from Titania to Hippolyta at the end of the play.

Weft visible through caul net.

- A commercial lace-front wig with synthetic hair would also work but the caul net may need altering. The instructions for this come later in this example.

Caul Net

Traditionally and historically, wigs for personal and theatre use were built with the top section made of caul net. Hair was double knotted on to this.

Wig re-blocked on shell to see where extension is needed.

Caul net on ladies' wigs served as a bag to hold the anticipated long hair underneath. The elastic nature of the net meant the wig would still fit, even if the hair were put up in a lumpy bun underneath, rather than being evenly spread around the head.

However, this allowed the hair to deform the shape of the wig and therefore caul net has been generally abandoned in media work. A non-elastic foundation to control the silhouette is generally preferred by custom wig makers and gives the option of full knotting or part wefting.

Commercial wigs are traditionally based on flexible, wide-holed caul net with a stiffer lace that circles the head to give the wig a snug fit. The wig itself is made of wefted fibre sewn onto caul net, and at the sides of the nape the lines of weft are visible.

The elastic foundation still has a place in street wear, especially over a bald head. Whenever time and money allow, it is best to make a new wig, with a lace foundation.

This style can be produced with a commercial fibre wig wefted on caul net but it may need some alterations. The commercial wig is often a little too small and will not sit securely on the head before you take tucks. To make the wig a little larger, add in a section of foundation, or base it on a larger foundation, custom made.

METHODS FOR ALTERING A WEFTED CAUL NET WIG

There are two ways to approach the alteration:

A. Add pieces to the existing wig.
B. Mount the wig to be altered on a suitable foundation that fits the shell.

Method 1: Adding Pieces

TOOLS:
- Shell.
- Block.
- Marker pens.
- Pins.
- Foundation lace to match wig.
- Needle and cotton to match wig.
- Scissors.
- Chalk.
- Hair or fibre to match wig.
- Hook and whipping nylon.

METHOD
1. Block up your shell and mark the centre of it as for foundation making.
2. Lay the wig over it to see where it needs extending. This is usually the temples and the sides of the nape.
3. Remove the wig and cut off the elastic at either side of the nape and the temple crescents.
4. Put the wig back on the block to see where the edges now come to. Mark this with a line of chalk, remove the wig and replace the chalk with a marker pen line and tape over it.
5. Now that you can see the extent of the problem, find some foundation lace to match.
6. Take a pattern of each section to be added by laying on cling film, marking the outline with a marker pen and taping over the whole

Re-blocked with lace addition ready to be knotted.

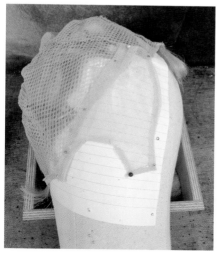

Interior of adding a lace extension.

section. Cut out the lace pieces to fit the pattern, adding 2cm for seam allowance all round.
7. Lay and pin your new lace pieces separately on to the shell. One piece on each side of the nape and the others each side of the front, checking that the dominant lines match.
8. Leave 1cm beyond the hairline on each piece and leave 2cm beyond the marker pen lines.
9. Fold the front hairline edge of the two temple pieces up towards you and fold 1cm under to make a neat seam; pin and whip this. Leave the other side of each piece of extra lace loose, laid over the marker pen line where the wig will join it.
10. Repeat for all four pieces.
11. Lay the wig on the block inside out, hair down, pin down and work on one section at a time, so that you can clear the hair out of your way as you work.
12. Line up one side of the wig nape lying on the marker pen line, lift the lace over it. Fold the lace down and fold it under by 1cm to make a seam with the side of the wig. Pin and whip this seam in two rows.

13. Repeat with the other sections.
14. Take the wig and lace off the block, turn the wig over and examine your seams. Often the join with the wig needs a little finishing off. Use needle and thread to hold down stray ends of weft. Sewing weft works better than trying to whip it. Aim for the middle of the weft's horizontal stitches.
15. Now block your wig right side out to knot the bald patches.
16. Knot the new areas; single knots of two hairs and double the knots over the seams.

Method 2: To Mount the Wig on a New Foundation

TOOLS: SEE METHOD 1.

METHOD 2

1. First make a foundation to fit the shell, using any method, but use foundation lace for the front section, not front lace, and make a seam on the hairline around the front edge where the cotton line runs.
2. Then lay the wig over the foundation

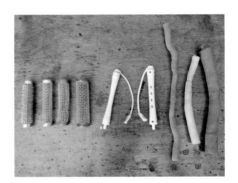

Selection of wire, elastic and foam rollers.

to estimate where it should be cut. It should fit over without pulling the new lace foundation out of shape.
3. If it is too tight, cut out the elastic section from each side of the nape. The usual problem areas are the temples and the sides of the nape.
4. The temples are usually extra strong sections with ribbon edging. If alteration is needed here, and extensions are usually needed, cut off the whole section. It will be faster to work on new lace.
5. Pin down the wig that remains and whip it closely to the foundation underneath.
6. Take the wig off the block and turn it inside out. Now block it up inside out, as tightly as you can, and whip a second line around the join of wig and foundation.
7. Whip an extra line over the directions of front to nape, ear to ear and temple to temple to keep the entire wig attached to the foundation.
8. Turn the wig right side out and block it up. Check it over, carefully freeing any fibre that has become caught up in the whipping. Knot the wig to fill in all the new bald areas.
9. Sew in the small combs that will hold it in place on the head.
10. Replace the elastic either side of the nape and take the wig off the block.

Dressing Titania's Periwig

The style is a mass of curls, an Afro version of the round, curled, Elizabeth I wig. If there is a free-standing crown, it may be mounted on an Alice-style head band of wire which can be pinned into the wig for security. As she is relaxing in her bower, it will be a circlet of flowers and leaves. This can be sewn in permanently or pinned into the wig each night.

1. The curls can be achieved with small

Re-blocked and ready to roller.

Front of periwig.

Rear of periwig.

Finished periwig.

The final look for Titania.

A drum skirt on Elizabeth Hastings, Countess of Worcester.

rollers, 1cm diameter and you will need about four dozen to complete the head.

2. Start from the centre front and overlap the hairline at right angles all round, so the curls will soften the edge all round the head.

3. If the hair or fibre is long, you may need to stack the rest of the rollers at right angles to the head, sticking up like a hedgehog all over, but if it is within 15cm you can lay them flat. For a tighter curl, try perm rollers or chopsticks.

4. After rollering, steam the curls or leave the wig in a drying oven for half an hour.

5. Let the wig cool before taking out the rollers and working through the wig, forming separate curls all over, and arranging small sections over the front hairline and longer ones at the nape.

The Seventeenth Century: History, Hairstyles and Plays

6

THE LATER REIGN OF ELIZABETH I

This is the age of Roundheads and Cavaliers, the plague and Great Fire of London, and the Merry Monarch with many mistresses. However, before all that, the century began as the sixteenth century had ended, with Elizabeth I in her red wig, still queen, and since the 1590s wearing the wheel farthingale stiffened with whalebone, to give her skirts the familiar drum shape.

Women's Hair and Fashion – the Drum Skirt

This is a striking and unexpected fashion, but once worn, all is made clear. The material of the skirt was lifted, spread evenly about the waist, pleated and pinned to the 'rim' of the wheel each time it was worn. This allowed the hem to be adjusted to hang just above the ground and this style gives an immediate feeling of freedom to the wearer.

The weight of material is held away from the knees and clear of the feet to facilitate walking, and the skirts do not drag. All a boon to an ageing queen and the other ladies who followed the

A bum roll.

fashion. Social distancing (two sword-lengths at closest) was in itself a mark of wealth and power and this fashion emphasized it.

Previous attempts at dispensing with the full-length frame of the farthingale under the skirts included the half-farthingale where the front remained flat, or used the padded roll of material, often called a 'bum roll' or French farthingale. Tied around the waist and sitting on the hips, it was used by any lady wanting to look stylishly large-hipped, but unable or unwilling to go as far as the expense and inconvenience of a frame. It was easily made from rags and maintained at home, even for the average woman, and gave the requisite lift to the heavy material of skirts whether worn for riding to market or waiting at court. It could be worn under the farthingale to cushion the hips for extra comfort if the skirt was made of thick and heavy material.

Sixteenth-century ruffs – an illustration by Percy Anderson for *Costume Fanciful, Historical and Theatrical*, 1906.

Ruffs and Large Lace Collars

The whale-bone stiffening and wheel shape is an echo of the 'supportasse', or 'under propper', a wire frame worn under a large lace collar or ruff for support. These huge lace collars and ruffs were beautiful works of art and expensive to buy and maintain. As they are so identified with the sixteenth and seventeenth centuries, they are a regular accessory in theatre but should be approached with caution. They hide the back of the wig, if one is worn, but require consideration when dressing the back of the hair. Hair may get caught on the collar and loosened. At worst, a wig may be pushed forward onto the face or dislodged completely.

> ### NOTES
>
> Her shoes are now on public display, flat or heeled, they might be soft leather, pinked and heavily jewelled like the pair revealed in a portrait of Elizabeth held by the National Trust at Hardwick Hall in Derbyshire.

LEFT:Queen Elizabeth I of England in red periwig with attached curls, standing collar. *The Hardwick Hall Portrait, The Mask of Youth,* c. 1599.

King James VI of Scotland and I of England by John de Critz.

KING JAMES TAKES THE THRONE

The arrival of James I after the death of Elizabeth I in 1603 made little immediate change to life. The population continued to grow and migrate towards the towns, mostly London, looking for work. Occasional food shortages from bad weather continued to affect prices.

The poorest were reduced to gleaning or poaching for food and sleeping rough, putting themselves outside the law. As they walked in a world where social position was something you were born into, but might aspire to better, the people they met were farmers, tradespeople, the gentry and the peerage, all concentrating on keeping their own livelihoods secure.

In 1563, a law had been passed forcing villagers to pay towards the upkeep of their local poor. This simply increased their efforts to speed travellers on to the next village.

In 1572 Parliament had passed an act 'for the punishment of vagabonds and the relief of the poor and impotent', which stated that a vagabond over the age of fourteen years 'shall be grievously whipped and burned through the gristle of the right ear with a hot iron of the compass of one inch'. A young man of eighteen who had been caught for a second time could be hanged as a felon. As a deterrent, this had failed. A starving, homeless person needs help, not punishment.

Not till 1597 did Elizabeth's government pass an act, revised in 1601, repealing the maiming of vagabonds and again trying to establish hospitals and workhouses for the poor, but as these were paid for by local taxes, compulsory and unpopular, to be poor was to be a burden to your neighbours. It was therefore ingrained into generations the importance of demonstrating your wealth through your appearance while outdoors. This would show strangers that you were not a vagabond and display to your neighbours that you were still solvent. Within the remaining sumptuary laws, regulating the materials available for clothes to suit your class or occupation, you would try to look your best.

Playwrights and commentators continue to mock the vanity of those who tried to dress above their station and deride the socially mobile – remember Malvolio's garters?

At court, Queen Anne favoured mostly the same styles as Queen Elizabeth I in clothes and hair. Wearing her hair rising in an oval beehive meant the other ladies at court could continue to display

Malvolio courts Olivia in his famous yellow 'cross'd garters' while Maria hides her giggles. An engraving by R. Staines after a painting by Daniel Maclise.

Queen Anne of Denmark (1605), attributed to John de Critz.

King James VI of Scotland and I of England with cropped hair and styled beard and moustache.

their hair wearing caps, veils, hats and hoods for warmth as required, rather than as some convention of modesty. Women who preferred a wig, to disguise a lack of hair or simply for convenience, could continue to wear one.

Most women continued to cover their head with tightly wrapped cloth or a neat linen cap, adding a hat or hood when going outside.

A fashion-forward move away from the drum skirt can be seen in this portrait of Marchesa Brigida Spinola-Doria in 1606 by Rubens with stunning fontange, extravagant ruff, but no wheel to make the drum shape.

By 1615, the wheels had gone from skirts, and hems had dropped to cover the ankles once more.

Men's Hair and Fashion

Men continued to let their hair grow beyond their jaws, but as we see with the famous Shakespeare picture, on the first page of the *First Folio*, a high, wide collar worn over a frame bunched up the nape hair.

Younger men gave up wearing a frame to support the collar or ruff, relying instead on starch to keep it smooth and let their collars fall from a neck band set high against the jaw, down on to the shoulders.

There is a lovely painting by Rubens of him and his wife in 1610. He has a full beard and moustache and his hair is curling softly around his ears and nape under a hat. He is wearing a superb lace collar, worn open at the neck and lying casually on his shoulders. His trousers are already long enough for his stocking garters to be tied beneath the knees. A wealthy, successful young artist in the height of fashion. His wife wears a lace cap under her hat and a huge cartwheel of lace ruff beneath her chin.

In 1616, Isaac Oliver made a portrait of the Earl of Dorset, Richard Sackville, wearing the thigh-length breeches of the earlier Elizabethan years with a magnificent lace collar worn over a

Portrait of Marchesa Brigida Spinola-Doria (1606) by Rubens with fontange, extravagant ruff, but no wheel to make the drum shape.

William Shakespeare with longer hair and wide collar from the *First Folio*.

frame, like Shakespeare. Changing styles took years to become established as more conservative and thrifty men hung back.

Facial Hair Fashion

Beards and moustaches were worn short and groomed. In a country where the general greeting was a kiss on the lips, the grooming of facial hair was a social nicety, as the perfuming of beards mitigated the smell of bad breath at close quarters. However, the use of irons heated in the fire to curl beard hair might leave a smell of singeing that not much could disguise.

THE REIGN OF KING CHARLES I

King James I reigned for twenty-two years, until Charles I became king on James' death in 1625.

Charles I in 1630 by Van Dyck.

Portrait of George Villiers, 1st Duke of Buckingham in tied falling collar.

Rubens in falling collar and Isabella Brandt in ruff, *The Honeysuckle Bower* portrait, c. 1609.

Waistlines rose a little for men and women, and hats began to be larger and flatter. For men, the hair often covered the ears, sometimes with a longer ringlet or 'lovelock' hanging down. For younger women, hair was worn flatter on top, drawn back to the bun, leaving curls on either side of the face. These were achieved by sleeping with their side hair wound in rags and the front curls set with spit or glue.

Less starched, with a neckband that reached the chin when fastened, the large 'falling' collar became an established accessory among men and women during the reign of King Charles I.

CROMWELLIAN FASHION

Later, during the Civil War, there was a more obvious variation in hair length between the Puritan minorities who wore hair cropped short and the others, even the Parliamentary commanders, who generally persisted with wearing longer hair, down to and below collar length, like the king. Afterwards, under the Protectorate of Oliver Cromwell, fashions continued as before, with longer hair

under their hats for men and curly side hair in front of a bun for richer women or wrapped in cloth or a cap, for the poorer majority.

THE REIGN OF CHARLES II

Wigs and hairpieces, even false beards, have been made and worn for thousands of years, generally in the hope of being mistaken for natural growth. They were routinely worn in theatres by the cast on stage and at court entertainments, mentioned by Bottom as he tries on different colours and mentioned in accounts of disguises and daring escapes from the Tower of London, so there have always been wig makers offering their wares, albeit discretely.

The ubiquitous hats for men meant that those who preferred could wear a 'border' or back fall of hair to achieve the fashionable length, or go for a full wig, which would be held securely in place by the hat.

Wigs had become so commonplace by the time of the Restoration, when Charles II became king (he was the Merry Monarch of publicly acknowledged 'many mistresses'), that he felt the need to forbid the clergy to wear wigs. They continued to wear them.

Charles II in Garter robes by John Michael Wright or studio, c. 1660–1665.

Wigs worn by men had become a comfortable fashion, warm and convenient, hygienic (easier to wash frequently and caps the head to stop the spread of lice) and stylish. Despite the expense, they would be openly worn for the next 130 years.

A Midsummer Night's Dream,
Act 1 scene 2

BOTTOM: Well, I will undertake it. What beard were I best to play it in?

QUINCE: Why, what you will.

BOTTOM: I will discharge it in either your straw-color beard, your orange-tawny beard, your purple-in-grain beard, or your French-crown-color beard, your perfit yellow.

Oliver Cromwell by Samuel Cooper.

Portrait of Samuel Pepys (1633–1703) by John Hayls.

They were accepted by clergy and clerics, officers of the law and the military. Samuel Pepys gives us the details of becoming a wig wearer in 1663 in his diary. He felt it was his duty as the king was openly wearing one. At first a feeling of reluctant curiosity, nervousness that he will be made fun of in public, the revelation of how dashing he looks in it, in his own eyes, then with compliments coming his way from colleagues and family, the need to buy more and bigger wigs! That year Pepys had the wig maker cut his hair short for easier upkeep so there was no going back. He arranged for the wigs to return to the wig maker for regular maintenance.

With no need to spend time dyeing or curling their client's hair, now simply keeping it short, the barbers trimmed and styled the gentlemen's beards and moustaches, which quickly became much smaller than before. Some began to shave them off completely.

After the Great Fire of London in 1666, King Charles II made a radical decision to regulate court dress for men. Their knee-length trousers would be almost completely covered by a long waistcoat, and over that a long coat. The new style was less bulky, more elegant, but warmer, practical and comfortable. Smoother shoulders were hidden under the hanging curls of the periwig. The large lace collar was replaced with a long scarf, called a cravat, wound several times about the neck for warmth, the ends could be a waterfall of lace, but by the end of the century were more likely to be plain.

While the men had been cutting their hair shorter to wear under the periwigs, the wealthier women had been having their maids embellish their front hair with added side curls for years, sometimes assisted by wire to give more fullness. This style is detailed in the 'Second Stuart Woman' example. The wig makers could curl these false pieces much more tightly than the rags did and there was no longer the necessity of risking burns with heated irons to restore drooping curls.

From 1671 a development of a French style called the Hurluberlu began to be fashionable. The whole front hair from a central break was shorter and curled, the back hair in a bun as usual. Ringlets of nape hair were brought forward to lie on

Sophia Dorothea of Celle by Voet.

Nell Gwyn, actress and mistress of Charles II with ringlets.

a bosom no longer covered by a white collar, merely a low fichu at the front of the dress.

To achieve this look, a woman could add switches and braids or an entire bun to make a more elaborate and fuller chignon, using her own side hair curled at the front and leaving her own back hair to become hanging ringlets. Alternatively, the whole wide, tightly curled front hair might be a false piece.

THE LATTER SEVENTEENTH CENTURY

When King Charles II died, James II continued to fight wars and uprisings and finally in 1688 William and Mary took the throne.

The East India Company was now importing more cotton than spices. Cotton was generally popular because as a fibre it was softer than linen against the skin, stronger and less likely to crease and easier to dye and sew. At home, a woman might dispense with the false hairpieces and wear a simple gathered cap, with pieces of lace and cotton lawn called lappets hanging down the back.

Under the cap, her own hair would be pulled back in a bun. The front hair, still on show, could be puffed up with curls, her own or false.

By 1690 this had developed into something more extreme. The short front hair was curled and gelled (possibly with hot irons and gum Arabic) to stand up above the forehead in a style known as the 'tour'. Behind the front hair, a tower of false curls built over a wire frame could be pinned in.

The hair could be topped with ribbons for extra height or just the cap itself could have a front section of upright lace in folds or pleats, to give the fashionable shape. Hoods were worn to protect the edifice outdoors.

Catherine of Bragança, Infanta of Portugal.

For poorer women, the head wrap, with or without a hat, remained necessary headwear for warmth, indoors or out.

Men's wigs reached new heights; there might be two mounds or horns of curly hair at the front of the wig and the sides and back hung nearly to the waist. The full bottomed wig, as it was known, was now everywhere. Top heavy and imposing, almost covering the face, warm as a cloak and hood. A fashion started by the king, followed by the court, this expensive item travelled down through society rather like a second-hand car. Old wigs were re-furbished and sold on. The old, discarded wigs were worn by poorer men under their hats to keep warm, during what was the coldest recorded decade in England.

Anne of Denmark with tour, 1605.

Anna Maria Luisa and her husband, Johann Wilhelm, Elector Palatine, from a painting after Jan Frans van Douven, 1708.

A BRIEF LOOK AT PLAYS IN THE SEVENTEENTH CENTURY AND THEIR WIG REQUIREMENTS

Small dressing tables and handheld mirrors had been common for years, but the full-length mirror remained an expensive rarity. People were unable to check the proportions of hairstyles and clothing when dressing fashionably, so some of the more extreme looks may have been a direct result of this. Equally, the lack of bright indoor lights meant that make-up risked looking garish out of doors. The result was that playwrights and commentators had for years been making fun of the unwitting victims of fashion.

These fashion failings give designers huge latitude, even in documentaries, and you may find yourself providing frames to extend wigs, extra hairpieces to enlarge them and hair or fibre of unusual colours. Be prepared, these are skills you will need to master.

Making Seventeenth-Century Male Wigs and Facial Hair

7

EXAMPLE 1: FIRST STUART MAN

NOTES

This is a poor, drunken ruffian, Pistol in *Henry IV.* An ex-soldier with no income or occupation except as companion to Falstaff. Although clearly a mess, he's vain too. Actor will also need beard and moustache.

- The need to be 'dirtied down', to look scruffy is key here.
- The wig is to be long and scruffy, to look unwashed, but with vanity, so add a bedraggled lovelock with a dirty ribbon.
- A straggly wig with a lovelock, beard and moustache will be pre-styled to look greasy and dirty.
- The beard and moustache are made in the same way as the Second Tudor Man, but the hair will be knotted more thinly, left longer and dirtied with gel.

PRO TIP

Dirtying down can be made permanent or temporary. Almost any colour hair will do, though blonde shows the dirt better. The Porter in the 'Scots Play', Stephano the drunken butler from *The Tempest* and Barnadine the prisoner in *Measure for Measure* could all use this wig after it has been styled if you wish to make the bedraggling a long-term feature.

First Stuart Man: Pistol. Similar inspiration in *Three Men and a Woman Playing Cards* or *Three Cavaliers and a Lady in an Interior* by an unknown artist.

Re-Fronting a Wig

Often, you do not have to make the wig entirely from scratch. Confirm a suitable hair quality, length and colour for the wig, then check whether you have a suitable wig already in stock. Even damaged, it can be more quickly repaired than re-made.

If you do have to start from scratch, please refer to Examples 1, 3 and 5 for instructions. Adding a new front will make the wig fit. Replacing the entire front lace of a wig is known as a re-front. It is a method that can be used to make a wig larger as well as adapting the hairline to a new occupant.

PRO TIP

- Re-furbishing and re-using old wigs is vital to keeping time and costs down. Never throw any useful hair or lace pieces away – they don't go off and it's good for the planet.

- A whip-on or mini-front is done by only removing a part of the old front wig lace and saves knotting time and uses less hair.

LEFT: A long Cavalier style with facial hair, easily adapted to a range of roles.

ADD A MINI-FRONT TO AN OLD WIG

1. Wash and comb out the stock wig. When dry, examine the inside of the wig to assess the condition. Patch and repair any small holes in the foundation lace or seams. Strengthen knots by gently pulling from the outside. Being thin shouldn't be too much of a problem, but you may need to even up the knotting. Consider a knot stop spray

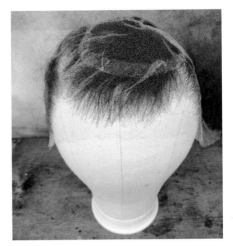

Interior of lace wig not in need of a re-front.

Interior of lace wig in need of a re-front.

afterwards.

2. Cut off any ragged front lace and broken lace corners, then even up the wig edges to look neater. Set up your actor's shell on the block and lay on the old wig, right way up. Check the fit all round.
3. Take the wig off the block. Lay a front lace on the shell, large enough to replace the one you have cut off and fit it to the actor's shell. Pin the lace down all round and whip the tucks.
4. Replace the wig on the block, right way up and pin down the back and sides of the wig. Pin the front edge down over the new lace at least 1cm behind the hairline of the shell, cutting off more wig if it overlaps the hairline.
5. Cut the hair for 2cm off the remaining front edge of the wig, as close to the root as possible. Use tweezers or depilatory cream to pluck out remaining roots.
6. Remove the front pins in the wig and turn the old lace under to make a 1cm seam with the new front lace. Whip down this edge, then whip a second line 1cm in from the edge for strength.
7. Run in your cotton line and knot the front, possibly using some of the hair you have cut off the wig, with matching hair.
8. Unblock the wig, carefully easing out the unseen pins holding the new front lace to the block and turn it inside out. Remove any blocking pins. Cut off the excess front lace and if there is a loose edge, whip it down.

PRO TIP

A depilatory product is a gentler way to remove roots from front lace. *See* Method in the 'Bald Cap with Hair' section, later in this chapter.

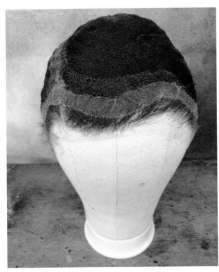

Re-fronted with double seam visible.

Styling the First Stuart Man – Dressing the Wig

1. A roller set will hold shape slightly better than pin curls. Use 11mm, 13mm and 15mm rollers, randomly mixed, but set them 2cm below their sections to avoid bounce and position them upright.
2. Leave some hair out between rollers.
3. When cool and dry, remove the rollers, working from the nape up

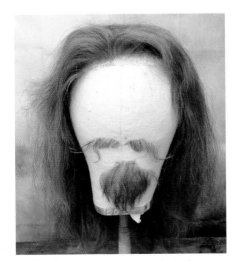

Pistol's re-fronted wig, ready to dress.

and pulling gently downwards, leave them in their ringlets as you proceed to the breaking down phase.

It is easier to achieve realism if there is semblance of style, so your newly refurbished, clean, combed wig should be trimmed to match the new and old hair.

Breaking (or Dirtying) Down

'Breaking down' is the technical term for dirtying down the wig and there are several methods. At this time, men of leisure would ostentatiously comb their hair and beards in public. In private, the washable cap would absorb some grease and using a dry shampoo of fuller's earth or flour, 'powdering', mitigated the rest.

As combs and hairbrushes were readily available to all, scruffy hair is a statement of just how poor and negligent a person is.

In *King Lear*, Edgar disguises himself as Poor Mad Tom not just by dressing in a few rags, but also by rubbing mud into his hair and skin. King Lear himself is soaked and blown about by the storm. In *Twelfth Night*, Viola is rescued dripping from the sea.

Required Effects

A. Wet or greasy. Wax softened by melting and mixing with mineral oil works well. Hair putty is a commercial version of this. A wet-look gel is a better choice, readily available and inexpensive. Glycerine or mineral oil are messy, spreading on to whatever they touch and their dripping is a slip hazard to be avoided.

B. Dirty. Adding fuller's earth or any other powder (for example, eyeshadow) will dry out the hair and read in the light as dust. Working on

Coconut oil.

Fuller's earth dandruff.

Wet-look gel.

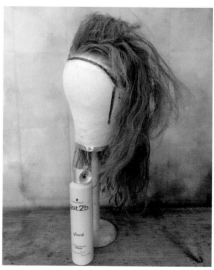

Hairspray and tousling.

dark hair, possibly locs, you may want a dried clay effect so mix the powder with gel or water-soluble glue. On lighter hair, mix dark water-colour make-up or powder into gel, or water-soluble glue, to look like mud. Using at least two colours in either effect looks more interesting.

C. Uncombed/windblown. Strong

hairspray and tousling with tail comb.

After breaking down the wig hair with gel, pull forward one straggly tress from the side of the nape and tie it with a dirty piece of ribbon to signify that it is, or once was, a lovelock. The straggly beard and moustache will complete the look.

The lovelock with dirty ribbon.

Final look for Pistol.

EXAMPLE 2: SECOND STUART MAN

Our Second Stuart Man could be King Lear, Malvolio, Justice Shallow from *Henry IV* or any other role that requires an actor to look older. We will need a foundation of fine lace, then a receding hairline of long, grey hair knotted finely so as to appear thinned by age.

Second Stuart Man: Falstaff relating his valiant exploits, George Clint.

To Make Thinning Wigs

1. Use the foundation-making information from the First Tudor Man, but substitute fine front lace in the top section.
2. If the actor has a shaven head or is

Front of lace wig with thinning grey hair.

Rear of thinning lace wig.

partially bald, use a thinning wig, revealing their own scalp under a fine front lace top section, or make the whole wig from front lace, making the seams with a single overlap.

Making a Curtain Nape Piece

A curtain piece of hair reflects extreme natural hair loss, sitting at temple level in front and dipping to the point of the occipital bone at the back. This may have sections of front lace in front of the ears and across the back and another section made of strong foundation lace at the nape.

The underneath and lace shape can be seen here, the nape pieces on the block.

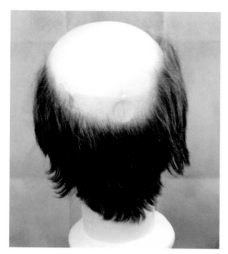

Brown nape piece on block.

Bald Caps

If the actor is unable to shave his head, due to other commitments, there is the option of the bald cap.

Bald caps can be bought ready-made and adapted to fit by cutting out the ear area and the nape. If the nape is covered by the hairpiece, the thicker cut edge will not be noticed and can be gripped or pinned to the actor's own hair.

Once the front of the cap is cut, that area must be thinned if it is to be stuck down and blended successfully. This operation can be done on most blocks, but not a soft cork-filled one.

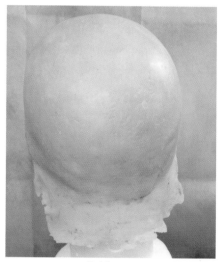

Bald cap.

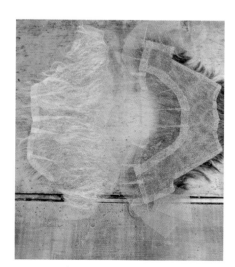

Interior of nape pieces.

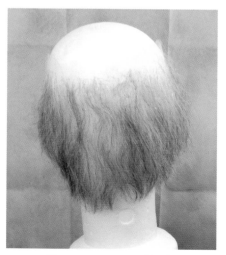

Grey nape piece on block.

Thinning a Bald Cap Edge

The bald cap may come with full instructions for use.

TOOLS:

- PPE.
- A block measuring slightly less than the actor's circumference.
- A parting agent so the cap will not stick to it.
- Vaseline or a cream made by melting together wax and mineral oil will do.
- Cool, well-ventilated workspace with hard floor.
- Cap plastic or Glatzan or a mix of the two.
- Acetone to bleed the edge.
- Two soft brushes and two small crockery or glass dishes with lids to hold the acetone and the cap plastic.
- A wig stand, preferably a floor stand, is essential.
- Talcum powder and a puff.

METHOD:

1. Check your bald cap on the actor or his shell and cut off the excess, leaving 2cm in front of his own hairline.

SAFETY TIP

Always use gloves with acetone. There should be no naked flame in the room. Acetone is readily available in pharmacies for removing nail varnish and so on. It feels cold on your skin because as the volatile fumes evaporate, they take your body heat with them. These fumes are highly flammable. They are explosive if the container is dropped. Acetone is a grease solvent that will dry out your skin. It is absorbed through the skin as well as by breathing in. The side effects are delayed by several hours as it moves through your body, but among others, the vicious headache is the worst one. Use as little as possible.

2. Place the bald cap block on the stand and wipe the front area, 4cm either side of the front hairline, with the parting agent.
3. Turn the cap inside out and fit it to the block, smoothing the edges at the front.
4. Put a little acetone into one of the dishes and holding it close to the front of the cap, use the brush to softly stroke the thick cut edges and thin them.
5. If you have inadvertently cut off too much plastic, or dissolved an area completely, you can add a little of the cap plastic to the second bowl and brush it on the block. Layers dry quickly but you will need three layers to do the repair. Avoid drips.
6. Clean any cap plastic off the brushes by rinsing in acetone and leaving them to dry.
7. Make sure excess acetone and cap plastic return to their original containers.
8. Leave the area and breathe fresh air.
9. Wait two hours for the bald cap to dry, then powder the new areas and lift them off the block a little at a time, from each side.
10. Lift the cap off the block. Lift the nape of the cap and turn it back to the right side. Place it on a clean block.
11. Make up the cap with grease that you have compared to that the actor will use on his face. Note that bald caps reflect light while skin absorbs it, so the actor's make-up will be too light to use as a base. Once you have made it up with this darker colour,

PRO TIP

Too much acetone or too much pressure and you will completely dissolve the edge. This requires you to rebuild it with the cap plastic.

add a little stipple all over to simulate the texture of skin. Powder with a velour puff to set the grease and knock off the excess.

Preparing and Fitting a Bald Cap and Curtain Piece on the Actor

1. Smooth the hair flat to the head with a water spray containing setting lotion, putting a setting net tightly over this and drying with a hairdryer.
2. Flatten the hairline more with a glue gel or Gafquat and dry with a hairdryer.
3. Wipe the skin which will be glued with a barrier cream or protective dressing wipe and wait for it to dry.
4. Stand behind and hold the cap with a hand at each side over the front of the actor. Lower it so the plastic edge of the front sits 3cm in front of their own hair, then ease it back a little until it is 1cm in front.
5. Ease the rest of the cap completely down on the head. There should be no dips, folds or wrinkles. Check that there are no stray hairs escaping at the edges. Put a hairgrip either side of the nape.
6. Lift the centre front with the tail of your comb just enough to insert the glue on its brush. Continue to hold the cap up while you wait thirty seconds for the glue to be practically dry, then let the cap sit into the glue and press it down with a pad.
7. Use the same technique to stick the sides.
8. Use grease make-up, at least two colours, to blend the join and powder off.
9. Spread a layer of glue over the nape and sides of the cap where the curtain piece will sit and wait thirty seconds till the glue is almost set.
10. Position the front before you slide the back section down into the glue. Now glue the front edges separately:

apply the glue, wait for tackiness, then press down with your glue pad. Use your tail comb to lift the hair, so as not to flatten the hair into the glue.

11. As the cap has been made up and the nape curtain positioned, it can be tacked on to the cap when it is taken off or just left glued on for succeeding performances.

BALD CAP WITH HAIR

To save time and for security, if there is a hat, the nape curtain may be fixed to the bald cap and the edges knotted into the plastic. A cap like this will be custom

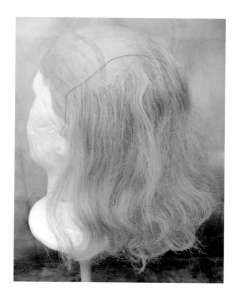

Laying our longer lace nape piece over the bald cap.

made and generally thicker than the average cap.

If your actor has a bald head already, the tricky part is done. Falstaff needs some length to show his status as an ex-Cavalier, so receding temples on a lace-fronted wig will work. You can adapt a pre-made lace front by removing hair.

Method to use a Depilatory Cream on a Wig

TOOLS:
- PPE.
- Depilatory (hair removal) cream.

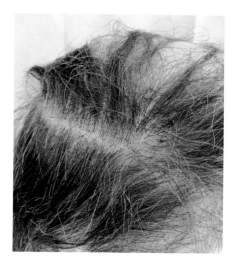

Bald cap with hair directly knotted in.

- Timer.
- Polythene bag.
- Old block.
- Large pins.
- Tweezers.

METHOD:
1. Unblock the wig and lay a polythene bag over an old block.
2. Put the wig on the block, pinning in the back and behind the area where you will be depilating. Do not block the front lace.
3. Spread the cream on the roots to be removed and leave the cream to work. After the suggested time, check with tweezers to see if the roots will lift off or need more time. Clean tweezers immediately after use on a wet cloth.
4. Remove the wig from the block and thoroughly rinse the cream off. Clean off any cream left on the block and remove the polythene bag.
5. Dry the wig and re-block over the new lace on the shell.
6. Check the area with tweezers to remove stragglers.

Falstaff's finished look with beard and moustache.

EXAMPLE 3: THIRD STUART MAN – PERIWIG 2

Third Stuart Man: Duke's periwig.

The third man will be the Duke in *Measure for Measure* in a full-bottomed periwig.

- In performance, a lace front on the actor's forehead, and combs inside, holding the weight, or a silicone band if the actor is balding, mean the wig can sit in its natural position, not obscuring the actor's face when he is walking around.
- Human hair wigs still need maintenance but today our tongs have thermostats and hair can be permed. So a lace-fronted, human hair knotted wig seems a good option. Wearing this extreme style allows his disguise as a friar to be simply accomplished and later re-established.
- These wigs were hard fronted and as easy to take on and off as hats; the hair underneath was usually kept short.
- This all works well for the Duke, recognizable in public by appearing in such an extravagant wig provides a contrast to his own short hair and makes its removal a believable disguise as a friar.

Seventeenth-Century Periwigs

William Hogarth's *The Five Orders of Periwigs*.

These wigs were made with human hair, whose curls drooped if they got wet in the rain. They were regularly combed in public but returning the wig to the maker for a full and expensive re-set with hot irons was the only way to look good again. A wig wearer needed a spare wig while the other was being dressed. More expense.

Photograph of Helena Normanton (first female barrister) c. 1930.

They were not washed, but likely swabbed with alcohol inside by the perruquier to reduce the grease and smell. Powdered flour meal, sometimes scented, was used copiously on the wig hair and helped to blend or alter the hair colour, especially if the irons had singed it.

We know from reports of their theft in the street that these wigs lifted off easily as they were not fixed on in any way. When walking, they were pulled well forward on the head and the heavy front ladders counter-balanced the weight of the full back hair.

When sitting, wigs were pushed back to the hairline or sometimes, indoors, removed altogether.

Making a Human Hair Full-Bottomed Wig

This will be like our Example 1, First Tudor Man wig, but the foundation is strengthened with a galloon on the seams, there is a flying nape and there are five added ladders of weft.

TOOLS:
- Lace fronted foundation as per Example 1.
- Making and knotting tools as per Example 1.
- Use 13cm pre-curled weft hair. (Avoid yak as it does not hold the curl well.)
- Galloon.
- Press-studs to attach horns to foundation.

METHOD:
1. Turn the lace front foundation inside out and sew the galloon (the wig maker's flat, nylon ribbon) over the seams for strength, by hand or with a machine. This is easier than the traditional method of laying a galloon on the block, making a lace foundation over it and sewing the two together on the block.
2. Mark the centre break and the crown with a cotton line.
3. Decide where the horns will sit at the front of the wig and draw two circles on the foundation around a 33mm upright roller with chalk.
4. Run in a cotton line over the chalk. Sew a press stud to the centre of each circle. Do not knot inside these horn circles.

5. Knot the crown area 3cm across in a starfish, but not reversed, as the crown of these wigs lies flat to the head. Use 11cm pre-curled hair. Pin it up.
6. Knot the hairline to lie back from the face.
7. Knot the centre break, 1cm wide.
8. Leave the nape section (N1) empty and knot the remaining wig lace starting from that upper seam.
9. The ladders are pre-curled weft 13cm long, sewn horizontally onto galloon frames.

Making the Flying Nape and Ladders

The lower nape piece of the foundation will have no hair knotted in. It exists to hold the foundation securely to the head. There will be a gap between the bald area and the hairy section above to help keep the wearer cool.
1. You need four ladders, 6cm wide and 28cm long. One ladder will sit in front of each ear. One will be sewn to each side of the bald nape.
2. Lay out the galloon rectangle on a

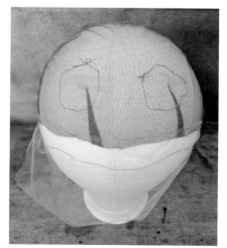

Foundation with cotton to show where not to knot for horns.

Interior of periwig showing the flying nape and ladders over the ears.

Pinning the galloon to make ladders.

block. Sew the tucks in the galloon at the corners. Add an extra strip of galloon down the middle of the length and sew it on. Halfway down, add another piece of galloon to sit across the short width. These rectangles of galloon will have human hair weft, 13cm long, matching the wig colour, sewn over them. The front two are covered on both sides. The nape two are covered on both sides for the bottom half only. The wefts are the rungs of the ladder. They will sit 2cm apart.

3. The flying nape will hang down from the upper seam of N1, approximately a square of 20cm per side. Make an outline of galloon, 20cm square, sewn at the corners. Add strips of galloon top to bottom every 4cm and across every 4cm to make a grid to support the weft. This weft will only be sewn on the upper side of the grid. The side against the wig will be bald. This piece sits on the shoulders.

4. Hanging from the centre of the flying nape will be one piece, the long nape, which hangs down the centre back of the actor. Make a rectangle of

galloon 18cm long and 13cm wide.
5. Add three vertical 18cm lines of galloon, 4cm apart.
6. Add a horizontal piece of galloon 13cm wide, halfway down. This

Ladders on the interior made with galloon.

Remove rollers and leave in place as tight rolls all over.

Attaching weft to ladders.

piece will have weft sewn on, but only on the upper surface.
7. Roller all the sections. Remember the double-sided areas need the separate sides rollering.

Rolled periwig.

Making the Horns

TOOLS:
- Two 33mm rollers.
- Foundation net to cover.
- Corresponding press studs to affix to wig.

METHOD 1: USING A LACE FOUNDATION
1. A 36mm circumference roller as the rigid inner for each horn.
2. Cut the lace to cover each one; it will be 13cm by 10cm.
3. Cut a circle of lace slightly wider than the roller and hem it.
4. Sew the other half of the press stud on to it.
5. Put the lace roller cover on the block; 13cm is the width of lace that will sit horizontally around the upright

Pre-curled weft for horns.

Lace and rollers for horns.

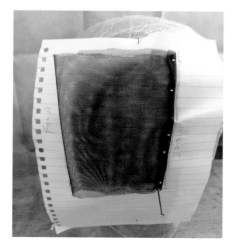

Lace-wrapped roller sewn on to the foundation.

roller. Fold over the upper edge 0.5cm, then again, 1cm, to give a neat edge, pin and whip this seam. After knotting, this edge will be gathered and sewn to make a little point on top of the roller.

6. Mark with a chalk line or pins, 1cm up from the bottom edge. This lace will be sewn to the lace circle beneath the roller, so do not knot it.

7. Mark a line at the sides with chalk or pins, 1cm in from each side. These will fold into a seam around the roller and those areas do not need knotting.

8. We are reversing the hair on the horns for extra lift. Sew a piece of weft 3cm wide to one side of the top seam, to lie upwards.

9. Knot the hair to lie flat towards the top seam. Knot 2cm, then sew on a line of weft.

10. Knot another 2cm and sew in another line. Sew a final line of weft onto the bottom chalk/pin line.

11. Put these two hairpieces into 18mm rollers, damp the hair with setting lotion and put in the oven to set.

12. When they are cool and dry, take out the rollers, turn the piece inside out

and whip down the sides to make a tube.

13. Sew the bottom edge on to the circle holding the press stud, folding in the bare lace. The press stud is now inside a tube of hair.

14. Turn the lace hair-side out and slide the roller in, gather the top edge of the hairy tube with a thread and sew it.

Styling the Seventeenth-Century Periwig

1. Before assembling the wig, dress all the pieces. Use 18mm rollers and setting lotion and bake in the oven till dry.

2. When they have cooled, take out all the rollers. Take the wig off the block and turn it inside out. Use a button thread to sew the edges of each wefted piece to the wig. They can be snipped off for re-dressing. Safety pins are not a safe option.

3. When assembled, put on a long-necked block to dress. Leave the curls in their roller sections and just tidy hairy edges. Use the tail of the comb to lift the hair of the horns into mounds. Coax the edges of curls slightly onto the front lace. Lacquer heavily all over or use a fixing spray. For a powdered look, spray lightly all over with coloured hairspray.

PRO TIP

Actors sweat more than most. It is a side effect of adrenaline, only exacerbated by the lights, costume and in this case, heat of a heavy wig. The human hair wig risks straight, bedraggled front edges. Fibre is not affected by sweat and holds the curl well.

Wrapped horns attached.

Rear profile of dressed ladders.

Dressed with black bow.

METHOD 2:

USING A COMMERCIAL FIBRE WIG
1. Buy two matching, seventeenth-
   century-style fibre wigs. One will be
   taken apart and the pieces of wig
   used to expand the nape and make

extra ladders for the other. They will
not need dressing. Use the method
above of wrapping hairy wig net
over a pair of rollers to achieve the
horns, sewing on weft from one wig.

Finished periwig.

Lace front grey wig with beard and moustache for a Lear or Prospero.

Making Seventeenth-Century Female Wigs and Dressing

EXAMPLE 1: FIRST STUART WOMAN

Our first woman's style is the teenage Juliet in *Romeo and Juliet*. This part was originally written for a young man, possibly about Juliet's age of thirteen years old, though these days it is most common to have an actor in their twenties play the role. One way youth is shown in hair with women is with longer hair. Another is to have lighter hair framing the face to reflect light towards the skin.

NOTES

In this production, we want a youthful appearance. Capulets all have dark hair. The wig will be for an actor who has medium-length dark hair but needs it to be below shoulder length.

Shoulder length actor's hair.

Santa Rosalia incoronata dagli angeli by Van Dyck.

LEFT: Purple fontange styles with rainbows for Iris.

- Hair extensions or a wig to match the actor's own front will be the best options.

Hair Extensions

Fibre ones are the lightest and easiest to maintain but real hair is always a better match. Extensions can be melted or clipped in individually, semi-permanently. Pieces of weft can be sewn, clipped or pinned to corn rows or pin curls or braids in the actor's own hair for each performance. Time consuming, but realistic.

Extensions will need tightening and replacing on a regular basis; again, time consuming and an added expense.

Hairpieces

To prepare the actor more quickly before a performance, use a hairpiece. Make a ¾ or ⅞ wig and use the actor's own front section of hair.

The method is the same for either size; simply extend the final lace closer to the hairline.

Three-quarter hairpiece wig.

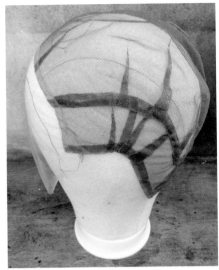
Side view of foundation.

Making a Wig Foundation with Split Top

(*See* Tools from 'Foundation Making' in Chapter 4.)
To make a wig foundation, use the same colour net as hair.

1. Follow the foundation making instructions for the First Tudor Man with the first three pieces of lace, but do not add a front lace.

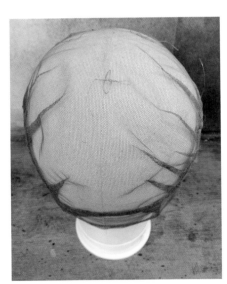
Rear of foundation.

Matching to find the right colours.

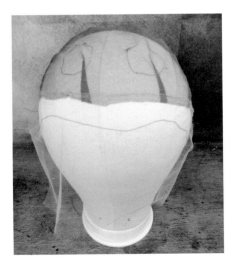
Foundation with dark lace for dark hair.

2. Take the foundation off the block and turn it inside out. Fold up the front edge of lace (N3) and whip it down.
3. Split the top lace (N3) along the line of the actor's natural parting, which you have marked with a cotton line, to just below the crown of the head. Turn the lace up towards you and whip the seam, either side of the centre parting, leaving a split about

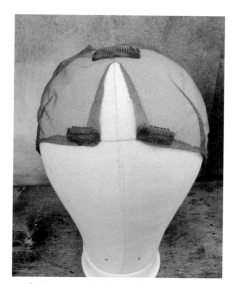

Split top with clip combs and crown comb.

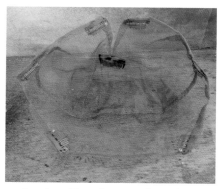

Interior of foundation with combs at nape, ears, and front and rear of parting.

2cm wide for their own hair to be pulled through. Both these seams are left with a raw edge to reduce bulk but may be overlocked.

4. Using a strong flesh-coloured nylon thread, join the two sides together at the front and halfway along the parting.

5. Sew clip combs inside on either side of the centre front split and in front of each ear and at the crown end of the parting split.

Sewing in Weft and Knotting the Hairpiece

1. Return the piece to the block the right way round to knot. Whatever the required final length is, there should be a gradual mix of the lengths of the actor's own hair and the longest length hair, and a mix of colours to blend with their own.
2. Use hair with some prepared movement in it, as this will aid the mixing of the two.
3. Sewing in weft:
   - For the first row, sew a line of weft around the nape of the piece before starting to knot.
   - The second row begins 3cm above that, following the curve of the nape.

PRO TIP

For a thicker fall of hair, sew in weft.

Sew in the lowest weft, then knot the space above it before sewing in the next row. It is always easier to take out weft than to sew it in amongst the knotting.

Sewn in weft at nape.

Next line of weft sewn in closer for a thicker 'shag' wig.

- The third row can sit straight across the nape 3cm above the second and nearly touching it on each side.
- The fourth row sits just above the

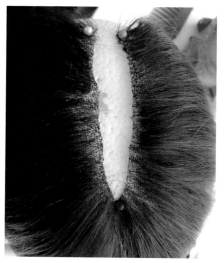

Split-top or U-part topper to thicken actor's own hair (this one made for a client with alopecia, hence the asymmetrical toupee clips).

ear to ear points, just behind the front seam so the hair can fall in front of the ears and across the back.

4. To style a club cut at the back, shorter hair and weft can be used in the nape. To hang in a more natural graduated point, weft and hair of the same length are used and the graduation arrives in their stepped placing up the back of the piece.

5. The knotting will be double knots of two or three hairs with three empty holes between knots, not reversed, no under knotting, and following the vertical lines of the lace.

6. Cut out the roots of the knotted hair as you finish each section. Do not cut out the roots of the weft as this will make them more prominent.

Styling the Hairpiece

1. Comb through and make loose pin curls in damp hair. These will hang below their root base as we are looking for movement, not volume.

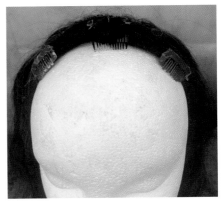

Three-quarter hairpiece with three toupee combs to attach in front of the crown.

Leave to dry in a warm place.

2. When dry, take out the pin curls and run your fingers through the hair.

Fitting and Styling a Piece with Long Hair

1. Leave the hair in the curls as they fall, not combing through, then pin them up in a few sections, so the piece is easier to handle as you put it on the actor's head.

2. Prepare the actor by lifting their hair at the parting and holding it with clips. Comb the side hair in front of

Hair wrapped with actor's own front clipped forward, hair flat on top with parting and plaits around the occipital bone.

Pin the wig cap at the crown and all around the edges.

the ears forward and clip it.

3. Make pin curls under the clip comb sites, either side of the parting, in front of the ears and at the crown.

4. Plait or pin curl the remaining hair, distributing the hair behind the ears and under the occipital bone. Often no wig cap is worn as the prep sits below the curve of the crown, but if the hair needs control, pin one on.

5. Position the hairpiece using the front of the parting section as your guide.

6. Move the clips to avoid the cross strings if necessary, then ease the back and sides of the piece down.

7. Clip in the comb at the crown first, then the combs at the front and at the sides of the parting. Finally, clip the combs in front of the ears.

8. Pin in each nape side of the piece by

Slide the comb in first before securing the parting clips, ears and nape.

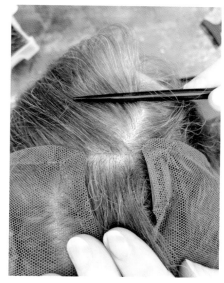

Combing the actor's hair to cover the lace.

and repeat with the backcombing and spray on each side and let them fall.

14. Return to the back section and gently part the hair and distribute it to hide the upper edge of the hairpiece. Spray over this with lacquer.

15. Return to one of the sides and check that there is enough backcombing to hide the edge of the piece, distribute the hair and spray. Repeat with the other side.

16. Part the centre front hair and use large curling tongs held over a comb to safeguard the face to make a roll going back from the face, all around the front. Pin each roll in a barrel curl to cool as you move to the next.

17. Supply the actor with a face shield for the hair spray. Take out the pin and backcomb each curl lightly and spray the underneath of each section with lacquer.

18. When they are all done, guide the top hair backwards and the side hair up to join in an up-twist. Slope the direction of this twist slightly down from the forehead towards a point centre-back, level with the top of the ears, and pin it into the piece.

taking tucks with one or two short, reversed hairpins (not hair grips). Bend the tips of the hairpins to go back into the piece so they do not get caught in the wig hair.

9. Now check around the piece in case you feel that a few more reversed pins would make the piece feel secure.

10. Once the piece is anchored, release the hair in the parting area and check the sections of hair are sitting either side of the strings.

Clipped on extension fall.

11. Hold the front hair section of the parting up with a clip again.

12. Take the back section and backcomb it lightly, holding it up at 45 degrees to the head, then spray the underneath of the backcombing with lacquer and let it fall.

13. Make a parting in the front section

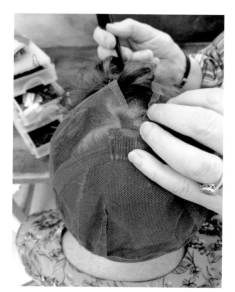

Pull the actor's hair through the nylon thread.

Twist each side and pin.

19. The twists will meet in the centre back and the ends can be held together with a small elastic, left to hang loose or made into a tiny bun or covered with a pinned-in ribbon. This twist will hold all the actor's own hair either side of the parting in position. If the actor's own hair is too short to incorporate believably with the length of the piece, or is not quite a good colour match, it can be taken up into the twist. The twist can be lightly gelled or sprayed with lacquer. There should be several small, fine pins holding the twists to the piece between the front and back.

20. Return to the front of the piece and tease out a few hairs in front of each

Finished Juliet hairpiece.

Hold each twist together.

ear. Holding small curling tongs over a comb, make a tiny ringlet each side and pin them. Look at the temples and if there are baby hairs wanting to come out of the twists, tong these forward as well. Lift the face shield and, when cool, spray each ringlet lightly.

Extension piece with mask.

EXAMPLE 2: SECOND STUART WOMAN – HURLUBERLU

- Doll Tearsheet, sex worker, and other women working in the brothel from *Henry IV*. The wig should look real, but she has attempted to colour it and the style is extreme – hurluberlu fashion.

- **HURLUBERLU STYLE**
  This style lasted as a fashion for less than ten years from 1671. It was replaced by the more formal early versions of the fontange, where the hair at the front was controlled and dressed up and off the face. The whole upper section of wide curls was often fake, the equivalent of the modern topper, and in the case of poorer women, might be second-hand and rather ratty. Their own hair underneath was left to hang as ringlets or partly pulled back in a bun.

  We will use the hurluberlu with wired side pieces and a bun on the crown as requested by the director, giving us the time period (though artistic licence will top accuracy).

The basis of this style is a wig with a centre break on either side of which the hair has been tightly curled, all round the head. The curls and ringlets cover the ears to the lobes. At either side of the nape there are longer ringlets falling forward. The centre of the nape hair has been lifted into a tiny bun just below the crown, nearly hidden in curls.

Over this wig, extra pieces of ringleted, wired weft have been pinned in.

Susanna Huygens' hurluberlu hair (1667–69) painted by Caspar Netscher.

The Wig

Four-piece lace foundation, hand knotted with hair 38cm long. A 3cm wide area back from the hairline can be knotted with shorter 22cm hair. There is a centre break. It is all knotted back and down.

TOOLS:
- Four-piece lace foundation.
- Pre-curled hair weft.
- 20-gauge floral wire.
- PVA glue.
- Cotton thread.
- Pliers.

METHOD:
1. Make the foundation and knot the wig as usual. *See* 'Making the Foundation' for Examples 1, 3 or 5.

Styling the Wig

1. Block up the wig, comb through gently and damp with water spray. Section the hair at the back of the wig horizontally, level with the top of

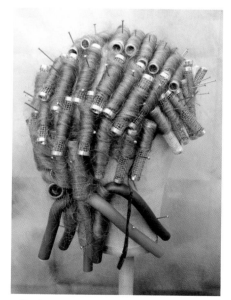

Hurluberlu roller set profile with bendy roller ringlets at nape.

- This sex-working character will be trying to look bright and flamboyant on a budget, therefore the colour of these false curls need not be an exact match to the wig underneath.
- The false curls can be padded underneath where they sit on the head.
- To extend the curls further, the weft that makes the curls could be strengthened with wire and bent to widen the look.

the ear arch. Pin the rest of the hair up.

2. Section off a 4cm square at each corner of the nape for ringlets. Roller that hair in bendies.

3. Put the remaining back section into 18mm rollers. These are sitting on their bases, not dragged and are angled up from the nape and in from the sides. This hair will be our bun.

Front view of roller set.

4. Release the top hair and section off the first 3cm of the hairline, the shorter hair. Set this in 13mm rollers, curling on to the hairline and following the shape all round, so at the sides, the rollers are sitting perpendicularly. They are sitting just on to the face.

5. Divide the break, front to back, as a parting and comb through. Use 13mm rollers set on their own bases. Begin at the centre front, beside the break and put the rollers horizontally, parallel with the line of the break, in one row, all round to the other side. Wind the hair to go down.

6. The remaining rollers will be set at

Bird's eye view of roller set.

right angles to the break, wound forward towards the face on each side.

Preparing the Weft

1. Block up pieces of weft to cover three times the temple-to-temple measurement.

Rollering the extra weft.

2. Take up a piece of the floral wire. It comes in 36cm lengths. Using pliers, fold over one end to make a small loop, bind this tightly with cotton, then dip the end in PVA glue. Treat the other end of the wire in the same way. Prepare four 36cm lengths like this and leave overnight to dry. Alternatively, you can solder the ends or cover them with sticking plasters. Whichever method is chosen, keep the little loop at each end free for pinning into the wig.

Floral wire looped and sealed with sticky plaster.

3. When the wires are dry, set them over the weft on the block and overstitch them to the pieces of weft.

4. Set the weft in 13mm rollers.

Pin the weft to the wires.

Oversew the weft to the wires.

Take the weft out of rollers.

4. Clip the top ringlets up and over to the other side. Lay the piece of weft in thirds, vertically onto the roots, over the ear to ear, and grip the bottom 4cm of the weft to the wig. The weft ringlets are lying up and over the top of the head.

5. Lay the piece of weft folded in four behind this, just behind the ear. Again, the weft strip is sitting vertically on the wig, the ringlets going up over the top of the wig. Grip down the bottom 4cm of the weft to the wig.

Dressing out the Wig

1. Leave the rollers in the nape corners till last. Take out the rest of the nape rollers, comb through and gather the hair into a hairband at the centre back. Twist this into a small, flat bun and pin it. Pin a hair net over it.

2. Leave the front rollers till later. Take out all the other rollers on top, carefully keeping the ringlets.

3. Take out the weft rollers. Fold two pieces of weft in four, bending the wire. Fold the other two pieces in three.

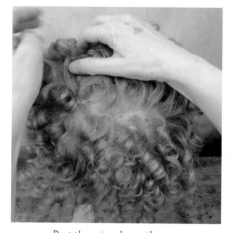

Part the wig above the ear.

Repeat on the other side and adjust.

Take the wig out of rollers.

Fold the wired ringlets into three.

Finished Doll Tearsheet hurluberlu.

6. Repeat on the other side.
7. Let down the ringlets of the weft pieces on each side. There will be a section of each piece that is fixed to wire standing out from the head.
8. Let down the top ringlets onto each side. They will sit on and around the wired pieces making the style wider.
9. Take out the front rollers and make small curls onto the face all round.
10. Take out the nape ringlets.

EXAMPLE 3: THIRD STUART WOMAN

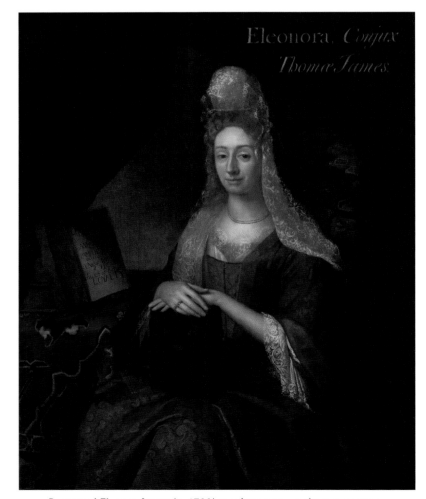

Portrait of Eleanor James (c. 1700) in a fontange – unknown painter.

This character is the goddess Iris in *The Tempest*.

- Her symbol is the rainbow.
- The fontange style is a tower of curls at the front of the wig, called the 'tour', built over a pad or frame to keep it as light as possible.
- A lace-fronted wig fitted to the actor's shell. It must fit well to be secure with the weight of the fontange.
- For the wig, use 26cm length blue hair, to reference the sky or purple for generic goddess. There is no difference to the method if the wig is

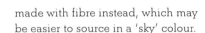

NOTES

Iris from *The Tempest*, wearing her high fontange in fantasy colours. The actor is also playing two other characters and this will be their final appearance on stage.

made with fibre instead, which may be easier to source in a 'sky' colour.
- Extra pieces of wefted fibre or hair will be added to make the curls of the tour, and ringlets to hang down from the sides of the nape. The rainbow will be a symbolic headdress of feathers.

The Fontange

In the seventeenth century, the hair would have been sectioned over the ear to ear and the hair at the back of the head would have been taken into a bun. This was a simple solution to controlling long hair, used for centuries. The bun still sits below the crown, leaving some hair at each side of the nape loose to hang forward over the chest in long ringlets. This bun would have been hidden under the cap.

The very front hair would be combed forward over the face. The hair just behind the front was used to make pin curls or plaits to support the base of the tour. The tour or tower was an edifice of curls, built over a wire frame or crepe wool or horsehair pad, pinned into the base.

Alternatively, this long hair surrounded the frame and was pulled up to the top and tied with a ribbon, securing the edifice precariously. Much fun was had by commentators at the time, at the expense of ladies whose tours slipped at odd angles.

The very front hair was curled with hot irons and glued with gum Arabic to make the curls stand up from the forehead.

Three fontanges in *Le Caquet des Femmes*.

False curls were pinned on to the tour.

The height of the tour is the distance from the top of the forehead to the mouth, assessed from portraits of the time.

Making the Fontange Wig

METHOD 1: MAKING THE TOWER WITH NYLON 'DOUGHNUT' PADS, 16CM HIGH

1. Sew together three doughnut-shaped synthetic bun rings of diminishing

Stacked doughnuts, nylon thread and Velcro.

size. The largest and lowest is 11cm diameter, the next 9cm and the top one is 8cm. These are lightweight and firm enough to carry the curls without bending.

2. Cover the tower in a piece of net, wig lace or even a plastic bag to blur the

Doughnuts covered in plastic of similar colour.

colour of the pads under the curls, and to facilitate fixing the curls in place.

3. Press studs are now sewn on to the base of the bottom pad and correspondingly on to the wig to hold it. Alternatively, you could sew the bottom pad directly onto the base of the wig.

METHOD 2: MAKING THE TOWER WITH A PLASTIC CORE, 16CM HIGH

1. Find an empty plastic container the right size and shape. A clean liquid spray bottle is ideal for this style. Remove the spray part. Measure the height and mark 16cm from the base with an indelible marker. Draw a line 5cm across the centre of one side at this height. Draw another line right across the front, 7cm below the first. Join the ends of these two lines with a straight line. These lines are the outline of the top half of the tower.

2. Working on a firm wooden surface, insert a sharp knife into the top-most line. Use strong scissors to cut out the outline drawn on the plastic.

3. Cover the plastic core in a 'sock' of strong wig lace, preferably the colour of the hair, and sew it in place. At the cut edge on top, pull the net as you sew, to hold the cut sides close together.

4. Sew a piece of Velcro onto a piece of wig lace and sew that onto the bottom of the sock of wig lace. Mark the position on the wig and sew in a corresponding piece of Velcro on the wig foundation.

5. Sew the curled weft directly on to the sock.

METHOD 3: MAKING THE TOWER WITH A WIRE FRAME, 16CM HIGH

TOOLS:
- 20-gauge floral wires.
- Wire cutters.
- A wooden board.
- Hammer.
- Nails.
- Pliers.

METHOD:

1. Find a core shape to work upon. Again, the spray bottle may serve.

2. Take out the spray handle. Use a hammer and nails to fix the bottle to the wooden board, nail through the plastic at an angle with four 8cm nails.

3. Pick up the first wire, they come in 36cm lengths, and make a small loop at one end. Lay your wire just above the base of the spray bottle, circle it tightly around the base and push the end through the loop. Tighten the loop with pliers. Pull the end up at right angles towards the top of the bottle. Put a piece of sticky tape on each side of the bottle to hold the loop in place.

4. Take a second wire, make a loop in one end, and circle the bottle about 4cm up from the bottom wire. Feed it through the loop and tighten the loop with pliers again. Pull the leftover end up at right angles.

5. This second wire is sitting over the extra bit of wire from the bottom circle. Fold that extra bit towards you from behind the wire. Loop it back under the wire to point upwards, tighten that twist with pliers over the end of wire in a loop. Hold the second circle with sticky tape.

6. Make two more wire circles as before, each 4cm apart, held with sticky tape front and back and with loose ends threaded under and over the wire above, tightened with pliers.

7. Take a new wire, fold it in half and thread one half of it down, under the bottom circle and bring it up to join its other half and twist it to stay there. Tighten with pliers. Thread the two long ends up to the wires above in a V shape, twisting as they cross other wires. Do this on both sides of the bottle.

8. Repeat with a new wire folded and hanging in a V from the fourth circle downwards, twisting and tightening as they cross each horizontal wire and bending the end into a loop. Do this on both sides of the bottle.

9. You now have a very lightweight frame. Unstick the sticky tape, pull out the nails and slide the frame off the bottle. Sew a strong wig net over it and sew Velcro on to the base.

MAKING A WIRE CAGE OR FRAME

This extends the height to any shape, used here for a beehive tour to hide a mic pack inside.

A hollow beehive tour with wire frame. This can also hide a mic pack.

Tour with wire frame from the interior.

Release rollers and bendy rollers from nape.

Styling the Fontange Wig

1. Sew pieces of weft along the ear to nape line of the nape. These should be at least 25cm long and will become ringlets.
2. Block up the wig ready to put in the rollers.
3. Part the hair 5cm from the front edge all round the front lace edge and comb it forward.
4. Comb the top hair where the pads will sit and distribute it in a starfish pattern over the site of the pad. You may choose to leave the area bald when knotting the wig.
5. Sit the pad tower on the wig to check the size and stand some big pins round the circumference as markers. This makes it easier to put in the rollers than with the pads in situ. If the area is left bald, pins are not needed.
6. Remove the pad tower and push in the pins so you can feel them, but they will not hit the rollers. Section the hair so the first rollers sit just inside the pad circumference, use 18mm rollers and sit each roller on its section.
7. Damp the hair and roll all the hair upwards, all round, starting from the top front on one side. Put a long bendy foam roller in the ringlet each side of the nape.
8. While the wig is in the oven drying, return to the padded tower.
9. Measure the circumference of the bottom pad, (for example 36cm) and triple it (36 x 3 = 108cm). This is the length of weft needed to make the curls for the tower. The hair or fibre needs only be 6cm long.
10. Block up the weft and set it in 18mm rollers.

Inside with ringlets of weft attached at the nape.

Assembly

1. When they are cool, take all the rollers out of the wig, except the side ringlets. Pin the front hair up in a clip.
2. From the crown to the nape, collect the hair in one handful, excluding the side ringlets.

   Comb it through and twist into a flat chignon just below the crown, centre back, and pin it securely. Add a hair net over this as putting the cap over it will tend to muss it up.
3. Let down the front hair from the clip. Clear the starfish area; remove the circle of pins. Press the stud of the tower in place.
4. Start from a section behind the 3cm of front hair you have pinned forward at the front of the tower. Take the centre tresse and lift it in a curl that comes forward. This will sit with its lower edge 4cm above the wig. This straight area will be filled with the front hair that is still pinned aside, over the lace.

5. Move to the side and pin a barrel curl whose top will be level with the bottom of that first curl, pin it to the tower. These curls are all about 3.5cm diameter, just as they have come off the roller, but as they may have been messed up when clipped away, may need combing through and re-forming. All the curls on the tower

6. Move round the base of the tower making curls, keep them as uniform as possible. The curls will be three rows deep above each ear and need hairgrips to hold them.

7. Return to the front hair and unclip it. You may need tongs to tighten the curls – you will need strong lacquer. Start at the centre front and make a tiny centre parting.

8. From 1.5cm behind the hairline, lift half the remaining hair to make a snail curl, one that sits open-ended towards you. Pin it to the tower over the straight root section left by the first curl. Repeat on the other side of the parting. The hair in front will be upright curls and curve on to the forehead. They will need spraying. The front hairline curls at the sides can be pinned or tonged to make smaller curls than the ones behind.

9. Take the rollers out of the weft, do not comb out the curls and cut off a 32cm section.

10. Pin the curled weft on to the tower from the side of your first and highest curl, round to the other side.

and sides should be the same size.

The strings of the weft are up, and the curl hangs down, like that very first curl. These weft curls should meet up with and sit parallel to the ones from the wig that are curled upwards.

11. Add three more rows of curls, working up the tower, pinning as you go with

Rerolling into longer rolls with fingers.

Pin in place.

Pinned roll.

Stretch curl to cover the tour.

Continue until the whole tour is covered with pincurls.

Pin in place.

fine hooked pins and tidying with
hairspray.
12. Add the rainbow headdress, the cap,
    and finally release the nape ringlets.

Dressed fontange.

Styled with rainbows for Iris.

PRO TIP

Take extra care to anchor the wig on
the back of the head to counteract the
weight of the fontange. Use big pins
rather than grips, threaded through
either side of the bun.

NOTES

This type of wig could also be
used for the goddess Juno
simply by changing the
headdress to peacock tails and
for Ceres by adding corn
stalks.

Styled with peacock
feathers for Juno.

Glossary

WIGS AND HAIRPIECES

¾ wig/⅞ wig – Missing the front as the wearer's hair will be shown and the wig will be attached behind the hairline, in front of the crown as a topper. It could be split at the top, the wearer's hair pulled through from the hairline to just before the crown so it thickens the sides and back but shows a natural parting.

Extensions/clip-ins – Usually smaller sections attached to the wearer's own hair or the wig. Can be clipped-in in numerous ways, sewn into corn rows or glued in.

Full lace – A wig with foundation made completely of lace, which is better quality than a caul or integration net and implies more hand knotting of hair than just sewing in of weft.

Topper/U-shaped hairpiece – Any wig which sits on top of the head. If U-shaped, this indicates a split in the top to allow the wearer's parting and hair to show.

Toupee – More associated with men, still a topper, but used to conceal baldness.

WIG-MAKING GLOSSARY

Caul – Netting used for part or all of the foundation.

Denier – Unit of weight that measures the fineness of silk and man-made fibres such as rayon or nylon. Equal to 1 gram per 9,000 metres. The lowest denier is ten, and is lighter and less dense with fibres, making it translucent. As the number rises, so does the weight of the material and density; 100 is thick and opaque. The lower the denier, the more expensive and more difficult to work with, but the better the result. Higher densities can be used for the back and crown of the wig, with lower deniers towards the front.

Integration – Blending together. Can refer to blending the client's own hair with the wig's hair by pulling it through the wide spaces in the net.

Monofilament – Monofilament material is a sheer polyester or nylon mesh. Most nets and laces are monofilament.

Postiche – Another word for wig or toupee, now most associated with wig making.

Ventilate/ventilation – to provide a hole for air to circulate. Used to describe the process of knotting hair into the wig.

WIG-MAKING TOOLS AND EQUIPMENT

Base lace – A cheap, durable material often used for practice or training before moving to German or French.

Film lace/HD lace – General terms for thinner and more ventilated Swiss or other lace. Designed to become translucent under the light of cameras, it can also be dyed. Comfortable but delicate.

Foundation – This is the base of the wig, which sits on the client's head. Ready-made foundations can be bought in different sizes very cheaply these days and adapted to suit, or you can follow our instructions to make your own, which will no doubt be lighter and more comfortable. More flexible foundations are more comfortable, suiting natural, unstructured hairstyles. Stretchy panels can even allow different sized heads to wear the same wig. However, the more the mesh moves, the looser your ventilation knots will become over time and with wear. You can prevent this with double knotting, a knot-stopper spray and an inner wig cap, all of which take more time. Stiffer mesh is less comfortable, but resilient, creating more of a hat-like feeling. Larger and more structured styles suit this foundation type.

French lace – Cheaper than Swiss, tough, durable and strong. Good for beginners and for larger knots.

Front lace/360 lace – The finest lace is used at the front where it needs to be least visible and most naturally replicate the hairline. The following are most often used for frontals or for a 360 frontal, which has lace around the full hairline including sides and nape, so it can be styled up. Different types are listed below:

Galloon – Synthetic ribbon with hollow core, which can coat wire for headdresses or keep lace pinned during styling.

German lace – The toughest and most durable lace.

Habotai silk – Available in blonde and brown, 100 per cent silk for partings and lining foundations for comfort.

Korean lace – Designed to mimic French lace at a cheaper price. It is more obvious than French, but good for durability.

Lace/hair lace – Not actually lace, but a mesh of circular, hexagonal or octagonal holes, the fabric of which makes up the foundation of the wig. The hair can be knotted in any place on the shape to create the direction of hair. Different types are used for different purposes and positions on the wig or type of hairpiece.

Mesh stretch net/Fine stretch net mesh – Blonde, Mid Reddy Brown, Dark Brown, Black. A stretchable durable net suitable for covering frames, prosthetics, bodysuits and so on, or for a section of wig. Always double knot the hair with this material to stop the knots working loose. The fine version is also available.

Natrilace – Available by the yard, thin, delicate, flexible, 30 denier, available in beige, it has a slight stretch and is slightly glossy compared to the Swiss lace.

Opera lace – As you'd expect, for use in opera and theatre. Twice as thick as film lace, available in different deniers, it creates durable foundations for its active performers on stage and is cheaper than film lace, though more visible.

Silk base foundation (silk top) – Used to create silk base closures, frontals and silk top wigs, which have silk material on their tops, this has a realistic resemblance to the scalp with individual hairs ventilated into it to create the same quality of hairline and parting as a full-lace wig.

Silky gauze base foundation – 30 denier, delicate, smooth and soft, useful for making natural parts in a wig cap and base closures. (Ventilating needles S-1 and S-2 are recommended so as not to damage or disturb the fine mesh.)

Swiss lace – Has a reputation for being the softest and least visible lace while still being tough enough for frequent use. Four matt lace colours. Durable and natural. Wide range of colours for different skin tones and deniers 15 to 40+. Potential fraying after use. Dark Swiss is available, pre-tinted for darker complexions for making full lace front wigs, lace frontals and closures. Extra fine Swiss lace – more expensive, but even thinner. Can be dyed with lace dye.

Ultra HD lace/HD lace – Among the thinnest and most delicate base laces available, transparent in colour, perfect for use at the front hairline. Can be tinted to match different skin tones. Least visible and softest, most comfortable to wear, but least durable. Perfect for photos, films and television, even thinner than film lace, blends well, tintable. Great for making facial hair such as beards and moustaches.

Vaniss/vaniss HD lace/vaniss lace ultra thin – Premium quality lace available in different deniers and a wide range of colours and lengths. Good quality, easy to use and becomes sheer with adhesive. Good for custom wig foundations, full lace wigs, lace closures, parts and frontals.

Netting

Caul net – Reliable, durable fabric for the back of the wig, covering frames and backing headdresses as well as integration pieces. It is natural and will dye using specialist fabric dyes. Not stretchy, but there is some give in one direction.

Crystal/smooth monofilament – Beige to transparent with square holes, used for making custom hairpieces, toppers and toupees. A breathable mesh, giving the illusion of a natural scalp, which allows for realistic ventilating all over, parted in any place. Or it can be used in patches just for the crown, visible parts and hairlines. Light, soft, very tightly woven and more comfortable. Available in a pre-made cap to avoid darting. Can be used with toupee tape (aka double-sided sticky tape).

Extra large integration/caul net – Available in black, dark brown and light brown/blonde. Large, 1cm holes, so useful for integration hairpieces. Not stretchable.

Hair integration string – Black, brown or clear. Available by the yard. These strings are used to create custom hairpieces or integration wigs.

Integration net (silk or mono) – A very wide netting used to make custom bases and wigs. Mono is flexible but stiffer than silk, keeping its form. The silk net stretches and is more flexible so must be sewn into shape. One colour. Can be used for pull-though wigs, aka honeycomb hairpieces or fishnet hair toppers which those with thinning hair can use to cover thin or bald patches, bringing their own hair through the holes to sit on top and create a more natural thickening.

PU/polyurethane/superfine skin like PU/thin skin – A slightly transparent 'Pale Blonde' coloured versatile plastic which is heat resistant, replicating the look of skin for the scalp for partings and breaks, edges, or prosthetics. Non-fraying. Also available in pre-made caps which need not be darted to create the necessary shape. Hair should be double knotted. Excellent for maintaining its

contact in water, sweat, heat or
humidity.

Stiff net/vegetable net – (£40 for 1m by
60cm) – A softer but still stiff net for
making wig bases and headdresses.

Stretch caul net – Available in dark
brown, mid-brown and blonde by the
metre. A stretchy version of traditional
caul net, useful for covering cages and
frames, inserting at the nape for comfort
and flexibility to fit different sized heads.

Stretch mesh wig cap foundation –
Flexible, lightweight, breathable for wig
caps. Six colours available. Tiny holes.

Swiss integration net – Large holes,
heavy but not stiff, sold in half-metre
widths, it is available in different colours
and is suitable for knotting and making
bases.

Terylene™ (Dacron™ in the US) – A
synthetic polyester fibre material, light
and durable enough for the back of a
wig foundation. Not suitable for the
front unless for a period, hard-fronted
wig. Available in any colour but
commonly sold in four skin-coloured
shades by most stockists.

Wefted cap – Constructed with wefts of
hair across the whole cap, giving a hard
front 'party wig', this is the cheapest wig
construction method used for mass
production. Front lace can be attached
to give a more natural hairline.

KNOTTING EQUIPMENT

Hooks/Needles

Asian knotting hook – The most
common type of hook.

German needle – Available in varied
sizes. Below 1 are very fine hooks for
single hairs. Fine hooks 1, 2, 3 are for
two to three hairs; 4, 5 and 6 are
medium hooks for coarse hair, two to
four strands; 7, 8 and 9 are for a lot of
thick hair or very coarse hair such as tail
yak; 10 and 12 are used for whipping
bases and foundations. Longer than
Asian needles, they can be used for
single or double knotting.

Knotting hook holder/grip/handle –
Different weights and lengths of handle
are available and in different materials. I
like to use a weightier handle as the
number on the hook increases.
Experiment with what feels comfortable
and keep different handles to denote
your different hooks at a glance or by
feel alone. You can also write the
number on the handle with permanent
marker or nail varnish. Some have
deeper furrows for extra grip, important
if you are knotting for long periods or
develop numbness. Brass holders are
heavier than plastic.

**Precision needle/whipping hook/curved
needle** – Able to pierce tough
foundations and easier to use on a
curved base than a straight needle.

PU knotting hook – Superfine hook for
ventilating PU material.

Punching needle – For slide and punch
technique, inserts a single hair at a time.

Ventilating/knotting hooks – Metal
hooks with a flat end for clamping inside
the handle. The numbers allocated

indicate, roughly, the number of hairs to
be taken at a time – 12 is for sewing the
foundation. Hooks are known for their
country of origin and some hooks from
one region may need adapting to fit
another's handles.

Tapes

Blocking tape – 7mm and 1cm widths –
Nylon, available in light brown and
brown. Used for pinning down lace
fronts.

Galloon and blocking tape – Tubular,
ribbon-like, elasticated, 0.5–1cm thick
and available in many colours by the
metre. This is pinned around the lace of
the hairline when styling the wig, and
strips of plastic can fill it to create
supporting stays/struts at the nape and
over the ears of foundations.

Japanese fine tape/galloon – 100 per
cent silk, dyable, premium galloon
available in blonde, dark blonde and
black. Use as regular galloon and for
underknotting at the nape.

Sticky tape – Translucent, sticky on one
side.

Toupee tape – Translucent, sticky on two
sides.

Translucent flat tape – 0.7–1.4cm – Pale
blonde and brown. Used to support and
cover seams on your foundation and
around the edges for comfort and to stop
stretching.

Other Accessories

Blocks – Head shaped, used to support
the wig as it would be worn for creating
foundations, knotting, styling, dressing
and display. Avoid wooden – a
miserable slog, requiring hard pins and
a hammer, just cover your soft, cork-filled

block with a plastic bag to protect.

Chin block – For making beards and facial hair on. Your second purchase.

Clamp/tabletop wig stand – Fits onto a worktable. Will always end up popping off during your knotting or styling.

Clear nylon whipping thread – Strong, secure, can be used with any colour of hair. However it can be shiny in the light, so ensure it is well covered.

Cork-filled/sawdust or soft/maleable block – Your first purchase. A good one will have well-balanced padding; even, straight seams; a pointed nape. They come in different circumference sizes but will often need extra padding to meet your actor's specific head shape.

Cradle – A wooden cradle supports the block and can sit on a table or lap. Indispensable for knotting hairlines and facial hair to get to awkward angles.

Floor stand – Weighted at the bottom with an adjustable height and angle of head, plus adjustable thickness.

Glass block – Can be used for making bald caps.

Glass head pins/bobble head pins – Easier to see among the hair and more support for galloon or wig edges.

Glue – Mastix Pro or spirit gum for facial hair and performance. Needs acetone to remove. PVA for invisible drying on roots for strength for example, or to keep shape of horns and so on.

Glueless fixings – Grips, toupee tape, combs, elastic straps.

Hair mats/drawing cards – A pair of toothed mats for keeping your hair organized and your root end clearly labelled. Useful if travelling or as a palette for blending hair.

Hammers – A small, lightweight one for getting pins into soft blocks. A heavy duty one for hard blocks.

Long-necked block – For styling and dressing and displaying long-haired wigs.

Long pins – Used for blocking up the wig, setting and attaching rollers to the wig block, pinning larger curls and rolls and dressing in general.

Pins – Available in different lengths, thicknesses and head types. Use different sized shallow pots for storage of different types and lengths of pins. Pin cushions can be attached to the wrist or table for ease of use. Use thimbles and finger protectors to taste.

Pliers – Available in different lengths of pincers, weights, and materials used for the handles. Experiment to find a comfortable pair for you to use when removing pins from blocks and so on.

Red block – 56cm – Can be used for making bald caps.

Scissors – Small, sharp for hair; large fabric scissors and probably some in between.

Sewing kit – Different cotton threads in bright and neutral colours for whipping temporary hairlines and attachments. Normal needles are occasionally useful for this work too.

Short pins – Used for attaching the galloon to the front lace of a wig before styling, to pin curls in place on blocks, pinning tucks and so on before whipping down.

Tape measure – Retractable, attached to wrist or loose in your pocket or kit, keep a 12in (30cm) and a 40in (1m) to hand at all times (often by cutting a longer one short).

T-head pins – Support the lace to either side.

Tweezers – Available in different styles, weights, thickness of tweezer and material of handle. Again, try some out for comfort. Useful to have both a wide, flat-headed pair for plucking bunches of hair and a thin-headed pair for plucking individual hairs.

Wig stands – Hold the block so you can work comfortably. Buy the most expensive you can possibly afford. See it in person or get the weight. The heavier, the better.

Yellow/silicone block – For making foundations on. Slightly squarer than soft. Works well for opera singers. Can be used for making bald caps.

References

Arnold, Janet *Queen Elizabeth's Wardrobe Unlock'd* (1988). Leeds: Maney.

Bate, Jonathan (Ed.) *William Shakespeare: The Complete Works*. RSC Shakespeare HB.

Corson, Richard *Fashions in Hair* (2005). Peter Owens Publishers.

Malcolm-Davies, Jane and Mikhaila, Ninya *The Tudor Tailor: Reconstructing Sixteenth-Century Dress* (2006). Batsford Ltd.

Morgan, Kenneth O. (Ed.) *The Oxford Illustrated History of Britain* (1984). Oxford University Press.

Schoenbaum, S. *Shakespeare, the Globe and the World* (1981). Oxford University Press.

Appendix 1: Beard and Facial Hair Measuring Form

MEASURING A HEAD FOR HAIR PIECES

Measure the face, ideally with a flexible tape measure.
Measurements in centimetres will generally suffice.

Take the measurements of the piece you want to put on the face,
unless this is yet to be decided.

You only need to ask for the relevant measurements,
for example F and G for a moustache.

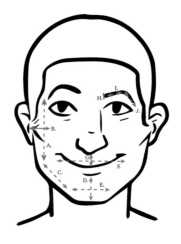

NAME:

CHARACTER:

EVENT/SHOW NOTES:

CHARACTER NOTES:

MEASUREMENTS:

A = ... cm   – Sideburn height.

B = ... cm to .... cm   – Sideburn width at top and bottom.

C = ...cm   – Jawline from widest point to the start of the chin.

D = ... cm   – Chin height from bottom of lip to lowest point of chin.

E = ... cm   – Chin width in line with the corners of the mouth.

F = ... cm (unsmiling) to .... cm (smiling)   – Width of mouth from corner to corner.

G = ... cm   – Philtrum.

H = ... cm   – Eyebrow height.

I = ... cm   – Eyebrow width.

WIG NOTES (for example structure,
style, budget, materials, style, colour):

OTHER COMMENTS:

Appendix 2: Wig Measurement Form

MEASURING A HEAD FOR A WIG

Measure in centimetres. If the wearer has long hair, this must be properly pinned up or pin curled, as it will be in performance, under a wig cap or stocking top before measuring. If this is not done the wig may not fit and may be damaged.

NAME:

CHARACTER:

EVENT/SHOW NOTES:

CHARACTER NOTES:

WIG NOTES (for example structure, style, budget, materials, style, colour):

OTHER COMMENTS:

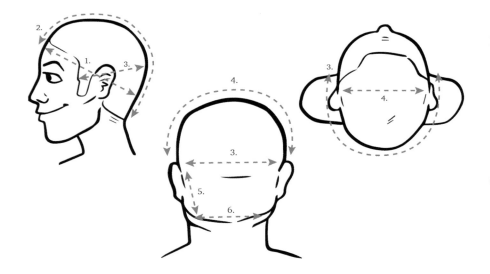

MEASUREMENTS:

1: C .... cm   = Circumference (measure all the way around).

2: FN .... cm   = Front to nape (measure from front of hair growth to lowest roots on nape).

3: TT .... cm   = Temple to temple (from front-most roots at temple).

4: EE .... cm   = Ear to ear (across top between edges of hair growth above ears).

5: EN .... cm   = Ear to nape (from measuring point for 4 down to corner).

6: AN .... cm   = Across nape.

Illustrator: Sophie Wright/Madebysoph www.madebysophart.com

Index